The Hidden You

What You Are and What to Do About It

Mabel Elsworth Todd

With a Foreword by Dr. Jesse Feiring Williams

D1601499

Martino Fine Books
Eastford, CT
2018

Martino Fine Books
P.O. Box 913,
Eastford, CT 06242 USA

ISBN   978-1-68422-249-0

Copyright 2018
Martino Fine Books

Cover Design Tiziana Matarazzo

Printed in the United States of America On 100% Acid-Free Paper

The Hidden You

What You Are and What to Do About It

Mabel Elsworth Todd

With a Foreword by Dr. Jesse Feiring Williams

EXPOSITION PRESS

New York

1953

Dedicated to the memory of

DR. JAMES HARVEY ROBINSON

—a sincere searcher for truth and a devoted adherent to the philosophy expressed in this book—in appreciation of much good advice and academic aid.

One of Dr. Robinson's wisest observations was "Of all human ambitions an open mind, eagerly expectant of new discoveries and ready to remould convictions to the light of added knowledge and dispelled ignorances and misapprehensions, is the noblest, the rarest and the most difficult to achieve."

Contents

THE HIDDEN YOU

What am I, Life? A thing of watery salt
Held in cohesion by unresting cells,
Which work they know not why, which never halt,
Myself unwitting where their Master dwells.
I do not bid them, yet they toil, they spin;
A world which uses me as I use them,
Nor do I know which end or which begin
Nor which to praise, which pamper, which condemn.
So, like a marvel in a marvel set,
I answer to the vast, as wave by wave
The sea of air goes o'er, dry or wet,
Or the full moon comes swimming from her cave,
Or the great sun comes north, this myriad I
Tingles, not knowing how, yet wondering why.

JOHN MASEFIELD,
Sonnet XXXVII

CHAPTER I

You and Your World

You are you and I am I because of many unseen qualities that make us individuals. Yet our similarities far outnumber our dissimilarities. Most of our behavior lies in the same category. Our behavior has been developed through the ages by our incessant movements toward survival in our world. This world has been changing and we with it, and you and I continue to evolve as we move with these changes.

Everything moves. Through movement the universe evolved. Through movement man evolved. The machinery of motion is life itself. To understand one would be to understand the other. Through observation of movement man has discovered nature's laws and has learned to interpret his world.

Life is a continuous stream of energy, its forces molding and remolding the inner mechanisms of man. Science has now produced evidence that man is composed of impulses of energy seeking balance.

The one great eternal is motion. Call it life, spirit, electricity, God—what you like! There it is facing you. Untiring, eternal movement—a constant search for equilibrium! There can be no fixity in a universe of such incessant motion. Movement is persistent, and balances must be struck.

BALANCE

Balance is a word of good omen, whether we speak of a well-balanced person, a neatly balanced bank account, the balance of the members of our solar system or a balanced national economy. The central struggle for balance occurs everywhere. All objects are related to their surroundings and to each other, and are in or out of balance according to the opposition of their forces. Action and reaction are equal and opposite. If we learn more about the opposition of forces, which establishes balance in all things, we may prepare for our own mental, emotional, and physical loads with more intelligence.

We meet inescapable change at every point. In fact, the only constant in life is change. This is the meaning of movement—the seeking of new balances as old balances are being disturbed.

Newton dreamily watched the apples fall many, many times before he wondered why they traveled earthward instead of skyward. In the cosmos there is no "up" or "down" as we think of them. We really walk on the side of the earth and are held to its surface by balanced forces. We would be more flexible if we got a "feeling" for this fact. We would not pound the ground so hard with our heels. We would accept the upward thrust of the earth and balance our forces to meet it. We have all noted this upward push of the earth when stepping off a curb that was higher or lower than anticipated.

New balances must be found when a change in velocity or direction of forces takes place, either within ourselves or without. One of our greatest needs is to understand our own emotional velocities and the changes they bring about in the direction of movement. Thus we may learn to *inhibit* less, to *guide* more.

INTERPLAY OF FORCES

All forces act in opposition to each other to hold the objective universe together. When an object seems to be still, its active forces are really in balance. The orderliness of the universe is due to balance in the interplay of forces. Before you finished reading the first sentence in this book, you traveled in space approximately nineteen miles. You do not feel this motion because all forces are in balance, and you and everything else are moving together.

We know that the stars are very active in their orbits, yet they appear to be fixed constellations because of their ability to keep their balance in the midst of the moving, opposing forces which hold them in place. Observing movement has brought us to the recognition of the forces effecting the shapes and positions of all objects in the physical universe. Heraclitus, as far back as 500 B.C., expressed a fundamental truth in the statement: "Everything moves."

You look at the Rockefeller Center or the Empire State Building or the Eiffel Tower, and believe you see designs fixed in space. They look solid and stable, but the amazing fact is that they are not fixed designs. Tall buildings sway an appreciable number of inches in a stiff gale. The Eiffel Tower expands with the heat and contracts with the cold to a measurable extent.

You think of this in terms of mechanics and physics, and as having no bearing upon your individual life. But universal forces operate upon human structures as upon inanimate structures. These forces make you a different size morning and evening as your living substances seek new balances to meet the strains of the day. With more understanding and use of the truths uncovered by science, many daily strains may be met and countered. Our strains are the harvest of the seeds of ignorance.

Movement in man is the proof of life. *Organized movement* is the proof of God's intelligence in evolving orderly behavior in the cosmos, and orderly movement in the highest form of life: the human being.

In the science of motion lies the key to better understanding. How do the forces maintain order in movement and continue to evolve? Only through science can man acquaint himself with cosmic intelligence. Evolution proceeded for many eons before man was conscious of it. Since man has become conscious of it, its progress has been vastly speeded.

Through movement man evolves. Positive, forward, creative movement! Try to change your thinking from negative notions, prejudices and phobias to facts as they are and a forward-looking use of them. Accept reality and build upon it. Learn facts. Accept facts. Accept your environment. Accept yourself in fair terms. Then you can learn to command your forces with a fair degree of faith in results. We cannot hold to our past fixities in the face of an ever-active present. It leads to nervous break-down.

WHAT CONTROLS BEHAVIOR?

Many complexities lie hidden in the problem of human behavior. How did we arrive at our present behavior? How do the forces of nature influence the behavior of our structural being? How can we better command our lives in relation to these forces? These are questions which it will profit us all to ponder. Upon our answers depend our relaxation and efficiency, and the spending of our energies with the greatest profit.

We have only positive or negative use of the forces at our disposal. We have only expression or repression. In the emotional velocities within ourselves lie the determinations. We may release ourselves from the bondage of tension by recognizing there is a positive expression for all the forces of life. We must find that expression.

To resist the forces is one way to destruction. Accept and choose. Associate more closely those stimuli from the environment which are helpful. Build upon them. The choice is yours. Give it attention by learning more about man. Many habitual tensions will thus be reduced, and relaxation, that fine active interplay and balance of parts, can be attained. In relaxation—balanced activity—lies the potential for greater movement. The resting cell is ready to work at a moment's call. Alertness is man's heritage. He must not dissipate it.

THE MATRIX OF LIVING SUBSTANCE

At one time it was believed that while science might describe the stars, the moon, the tides and the earth, it could never depict man. But since then his structure and functions have been laid bare, his living substance has been analyzed. Through the ages, as scientific techniques developed, tissues and cells came under observation. The matrix of living substance—protoplasm—is found in every living cell.

The history of man's movements and determinations lies in his bones, muscles and blood—in his cellular matrix out of which he developed into what he is. Although man can never be explained as a collection of cells, he cannot be explained by omitting the cellular basis of his development.

THE SCIENTIFIC SPIRIT

Since today science offers us many facts concerning our own forces, balances, and imbalances, a new way of thinking is called for about the substance of which we are composed and our management of it. Even knowing the facts does not make it easy for us to change old ways of thinking or to give up preconceived ideas. The scientific spirit and attitude, however, promise the best results. They demand a basis of *verified truth* as opposed to prejudices, opinions, and notions.

To change our thinking! To incorporate into our feelings the findings of modern science! These are the two ways to determine the ultimate release of nerve strain and a freer activity of those tiny members of our large community of servants—the living cells—of which our bodies are composed.

Science analyzes and separates. It opens the book of natural phenomena to the knowledge of man. To synthesize these facts, to pull them together for the purpose of more intelligent living, is then the task of every individual. The more intelligence that is applied, the more perfect is the cooperation of the cellular units!

Science has given us the machine age, the atom bomb; it has opened our eyes to the oneness of life, to the eternal movement and balance of all parts, and parts of parts. Understanding all this has brought us closer to the heart of the universe and to nature's forces. Better application to our own lives is the missing link.

OUR TOOLS OF LIFE

What are our tools of life? The substance and forces of the physical universe—air, light, water, heat, food, and structures. Also, the substances and forces of our own cellular being, such as bones, muscles, ideas, emotions, movements, and combinations of all these which serve us in our daily activities. The more we know about the tools of living, the more intelligent we will be in their use.

These tools are ever present and inject an incessant urge into our waking hours. If we are not employing them for our use, they are buffeting us about disastrously. Among our acquaintances we can find many who, through misunderstanding and lack of command of the tools at hand, suffer imbalances—mental, spiritual, and physical—with no clear comprehension of what is happening to them.

In all these human calamities, the forces which should be ready tools are rioting among sensitive mechanisms under no intelligent command. Better use of knowledge at hand is the only safe recourse. Accept the forces and try to understand them. Above all accept yourself and realize that you are in the same category with all others, even though you fancy yourself to be different.

You will then become sensitive to the way forces of the environment and forces from within you are acting upon you, and you will better understand your own emotional reactions to them. Thus you will gain a command over your own forces, and your environment will have less control over you.

Forces of nature, forces of environment—these are the two sets of forces involved in the control of human behavior. Do you command the forces or do they control you? Here lies the question. To command them you must accept them, understand them, and learn to use them toward a reduction of the strains of living.

THE SIGNIFICANCE OF THE "OLD" IN THE "NEW"

All that we are today reflects not only yesterday but eons of yesterdays. That which remains of the past to influence and control our thought and action is what makes it dangerous—and real. The past is not content to become merely what has been; it is always coming up to us, it is part of us and we are born of its life.

There is nothing new under the sun. All was there in the beginning. There is only new discovery and realization of the significance of the old. The so called "new" grows out of the past as the oak grows from the acorn, for it is being conditioned and reconditioned by the environment in which it develops. Our cooperation with the best in the "old" and with discovered facts in the "new" is needed for further progress.

Progress consists in incorporating the past into our present and consciously building upon it. To understand nature, to go with it and to guide it is our way to command forces about us. This does not refute the spiritual side of our guidance. One of its aspects, inspiration, leads to the highest form of self-development.

Our only means of self-control with a minimum of strain lies in adjusting the inherent natural forces to the outer environment more quickly. We must hold less, adjust more. When there is more movement there is less tension. The human animal, like all other animals, was forward-looking in his survival efforts. All the focus for movement in escape or challenge was toward the head end of the animal. If he backed up or remained frozen in his tracks through inhibitions, he did not survive.

You, a lover of freedom, find yourself in a complicated world surrounded by controls which you must understand if you are to make more successful adaptations for survival. At any moment of life, at this moment as you read, you are the sum total of all that has gone before, coordinated with the present balance of your organism and with the stimuli which come to you from your present surroundings—a dynamic mosaic.

CHOICES IN BEHAVIOR

We frequently hear the admonition, "just be normal, do things in a normal or natural way." How do we judge the normal or natural? It may be merely our *habitual* way. This varies widely in individuals. We cannot say that any mechanism is natural in its functioning until we understand the laws governing it. Only then can we determine whether or not the habits of the mechanism are in accord with its intended functioning; whether it is "naturally" or artificially controlled.

If we think of the behavior of things and forces as well as of living people, we will realize that everything behaves according to the effects of other things upon it. The things in the room in which you sit behave according to the forces acting upon them—the chair you sit upon changes its molecular behavior because of the heat and weight of your body. There would be another change in both the chair and yourself if, by some magic, the four-legged chair could suddenly become a three-legged one. A readjustment to new strains in both the chair and in yourself would take place. A constant struggle for equilibrium exists between molecules, atoms, and forces in all phases of nature and life, whether we are conscious of it or not.

SELF-VOLITION

Self-volition is overshadowed by an individual's physiological equipment, which has suitable mechanisms to carry out orders. You move or I move as these mechanisms determine. The brain may command, the muscles respond, but our reflexes measure the time and energy and organize the responses. The parts moving and the directions they take may fall within the scope of conscious decision, but the velocities and the organization are adjusted in the unconscious, and are automatic. Brain cells, nerve cells, and muscle cells accelerate and organize all human responses in cooperation. A unit inseparable!

OUR LIVING SUBSTANCE

The origin of the human tissues, their growth and development, the physics and chemistry of their composition, their forms and relationships, their physiological functions and the agents that move them, all lie in the cells. The orchestration of these intelligences is the integration of the individual. The salient characteristic of living protoplasm is constant cellular activity, with its ceaseless chemical change.

To our limited sensory mechanism there is the false impression of solidity and fixity, and this impression is difficult to erase. On the contrary, incessant change and cell individualism are constant. By becoming more aware of these changes we may assume intelligent responsibility for them. Constructive or destructive habits of thought and emotion may be discovered and rectified.

Our ancestral background is responsible for the development of our many highly specialized systems to meet the increasing complexity of life. Today our organisms must meet competition, speed, high standards, overstimulation, high pressure, noise, and gas-contaminated air. Larger numbers of people than ever before are confined in offices, schools, factories and various institutions for many hours a day; all striving to live up to certain requirements irrespective of individual differences in equipment and temperament. Biological and biochemical factors, electrical, mechanical and psychological factors, are all taking part in this moving picture of our lives.

THOUGHT DESIGN

Ideas, sensations, prejudices, misconceptions, ideals, and fears have all, singly or together, been heroes or villains in the absorbing drama of our lives. They have acted as stimuli from the beginning of our lives to the present. They have either been speeding up the action or putting on the brakes—all lending color to our interpretation of living situations. They have been the controlling factors in the reactions which have become our own particular set of habits and by which our personalities have come to be recognized as those of distinctive individuals.

Our bodies consist of a tremendous and astounding number of operations and activities which tend to cooperate in a single elaborate process, to which all the lesser processes contribute. This scientists call "organization" or "integration." That we act as a whole and in response to our sensations, feelings, thoughts, and memories makes what we *entertain in our imagination* important. Do we entertain constructive, forward-moving pictures of action? If so, this serves as a positive force, building reserves for our future use. Brain cells as well as muscle cells improve with use, not disuse.

If in the imagination we entertain hesitant, self-doubting thoughts, we waste energy in confusion. Our responses produce both mental and physical depression. This drains human reserves, and the ability to organize new reserves ready for use is dissipated.

The nerves, both motor and sensory, ramify and serve every minute part of the body. The glands, directly and indirectly, exert a powerful influence on our entire physical being, and together with our thinking, determine our individual behavior and accomplishment. Waking or sleeping, night or day, this interplay between our psychological powers and our physiological processes is incessant.

We react to what we think about. Our choices are important. If you have an undesired habit of thinking or of emotional reaction, choose the opposite and repeat this response until you have replaced the negative reaction by a positive one. Change the *action*, do not try to change the emotion. Emotion lies in the unconscious mechanisms serving the survival urge. It drives to action. You cannot change it. On the other hand, by persistently attending to the desired action in the imagination the undesired emotion will fade into the background. Satisfaction will finally accrue through accomplishment and the emotion accompanying the undesirable behavior will dull.

For example, if daily irritations are your lot, smile in the midst of them whether you feel like it or not. The smile will outwear the scowl in time. Think action, and action will take place. Do not try to inhibit the desire to frown. When inhibition is the emphasis, the result is uncertain. Confusions between mental and moral interpretations and emotional urges are sure to affect the outcome. Guilt will be felt but no good will come of it. Physiological changes must be made to effect a cure. New actions must be set up. Cellular balances result.

Your responses in small matters, day by day, will set the pattern by which you will act when the direction and velocities of your own forces and forces about you are increased. Note the difference in behavior of individuals in the midst of catastrophes. Satisfactory behavior occurs only as satisfactory habits of action have been integrated into daily thinking and doing. Established habits will determine your future reactions and emotional satisfactions.

The view that the organism responds as a whole to a wide variety of sensory impulses is not a mental, physical, or spiritual philosophy. It is simply recognition of the *fact* that this is the way our organisms respond. Philosophers for centuries have spun elaborate theories about the matter, and have wasted reams of good paper with intricate analyses of monism, of realism, and of historical dualism. But the facts are now clear. The human body is a cooperative community, working in harmony as long as natural balances are preserved and balanced relationship of parts maintained. Cells, tissues, organs, and systems are so arranged and so precisely interrelated as to serve the whole intelligently. This is the essence of unity—the harmonious relationship of cells, varied as they are in structural form, that establishes and maintains the integrity of the organism!

CHAPTER II

Our Strains

You and I have developed and found daily expression through the influence of two sets of controlling forces, the emotional and the physical. These play upon our living substance as the violinist plays upon the strings of his instrument. Every atom, every cell, responds to emotional and physical forces, inherited and environmental, whether we like it or not. Our heredity and environment include all that is within and all that is without ourselves. We are affected by both at all times.

In muscles, nerves, and bones our inner forces continually adjust to the external forces. Reducing the strains of daily conflict between these unconscious controls is our incessant problem. These forces must be intelligently guided; they cannot be safely inhibited. Then they are only buried deeper to spring forth another day.

OVERCOMING STRAINS

How do we behave emotionally under strain? How do we behave structurally under strain? Do we walk down the street with ease? Do we rest when at work or do we work hardest when at rest?

Have you thought much about these matters? Do you know how you behave? Except for the social amenities, most of us do not give our general behavior much thought. We are more concerned with that of others and how their behavior affects us, ignoring the fact that others' reactions are often the reflection of the impressions produced by our own behavior. To understand the behavior of others, we must first investigate our own behavior.

What are we doing about the daily problems that irritate us? If we habitually meet our daily problems with irritation, this will show in our behavior in spite of all efforts to conceal it. Our hidden emotions will break out when we least expect them to. They have been building up. If we continue to push them down, increasing our ability to inhibit, emotional and structural maladjustments are sure to overtake us; even gastrointestinal ulcers may result, or equally uncomfortable nervous disorders.

When our tensions become extreme we call upon our physician. We take his pills for indigestion, heart palpitation, the "jitters," sleeplessness, headaches, backaches. He may tell us the cause of our trouble is "nerves"—emotional disturbance, fatigue. Invariably he advises "rest," "let go," "take it easy," "don't hang on so hard." But we ask, "How? Why am I this way? What causes this?" And we receive various answers.

Most of us have grown up giving little consideration to the process of our development. Attaining extraneous things and reaching goals has seemed more important than knowing ourselves; but prisons and asylums are mute witnesses to the fact that not many people have successfully learned the full use of their God-given powers.

But do we want to change? It is a human tendency to dislike change; to resist it; to cling to the familiar in the matter of ideas, conceptions, feelings, ideals. For this reason, conceptions when well entrenched are seldom changed without a struggle. Standards have been set up by people and organizations—standards educational, mental, behavioristic, religious. Most of us give them blind allegiance. It requires daring to think for oneself. It is so much easier to thumb a ride on the thought waves of others than to blaze a trail along the markings of science. Our mental laziness may be due largely to confusion. We have never cleared the way for straight thinking. Such thinking requires facts and emancipation from prejudices, thinking freed from emotional sets.

From early childhood we have been satisfied with reasons passed on to us as to *why* things behave as they do. It often requires a hard bump for us to discover *how* they behave. And this proves true in both the physical and the mental realms. It is time we asked ourselves "how" instead of "why" about the behavior of people and things. When we know the facts about the drive of emotional and physical forces, we may be more intelligent in guiding our lives.

RELAXATION AND CONSERVATION OF ENERGY

The most mystical and important power at your disposal is energy. In man, as in other animals, this energy is generated within the body for individual use. The difference between the use you have made of your energy and the use that the other animals has made of theirs has brought about a great difference between you and them, although there is much you have in common. You have used this energy to increase your capacities and your understanding of the world about you. Understanding and utilizing the natural forces inherent within this energy has helped you to develop the power to overcome the limitations of your inheritance and of your surroundings.

Animals developed through the trial-and-error method. You have also developed through the trial-and-error method— plus the ability to reason, to apply logic to learning. Both you and the animals have the power of memory, but you have the ability to reach into the past, to recall and interpret it. You have the added gift of the power of imagination. This enters into every act of life, from the smallest to the greatest. Our every act is assembled in the imagination before it becomes organized behavior. This is accomplished by many stimuli in coordination, *preparing us for our responses.* If a thing is within the compass of your imagination, you can motivate toward it, and it becomes your behavior if it lies within your capacities.

Several things are important to the ease of living. We must let our bones rest completely on the chair, bed, or couch as we sit or lie. Do you know the reason why? What are the facts? We must entertain factual knowledge in the imagination. When we understand how human behavior is developed and how important conservation of energy is to survival, we discover new ways of correcting those habits which produce our daily strains.

PHASES OF MOVEMENT

Relaxation is a *phase of movement*. It is demonstrated in every organ and muscle of the body and, to utilize best our physical energies in the operation of our daily lives, we should try to understand how faith, confidence, and relaxation operate for conservation and serenity. Both conservation and serenity come through *balance*.

The best way to meet our inner conflicts and disappointments is to understand that the physical, emotional, and spiritual act as one in bodily expression. That is, the drive for action and the feeling for the drive, and the physical channels through which they flow, manifest as behavior.

"Two plus two are four" means nothing to a child as an abstraction, but when he learns to count his marbles he has the feeling for the fact and the urge to use it.

Relaxation is a phase of bodily rhythms and must be understood as such. And faith is the inner acceptance of our ability to perform the necessary acts of life. The faith employed may be but the unconscious faith that we daily employ in our confidence in living. For example, when climbing a flight of stairs while conversing with a friend, we may change to walking on the level without giving conscious thought to the adjustments taking place in the shifting of the numerous body weights. Our faith in the "older and smarter man inside" is taking care of us. This is but one instance of the unknowing, unconscious behavior which we trust in all our daily activities. We never fear that we may eat more of our tongue than of the beefsteak, nor that we will stumble over our own feet when walking.

If we understood the support of our body framework, we would spend less energy in the muscles staticly gripping our bones, holding them out of balance, and give more freedom to the muscles for movement of the bones. When we understand that *all tension lies in muscles,* whether from emotional imbalance or bone imbalance, we will find a more intelligent solution to our tension problems.

What is relaxation? How many of us have given the question of what it is much consideration? We desire it, but most of us have thought of it only as "letting go." Taking time out of a busy life to train the living mechanism habituated to movement to "let go" may be the quickest way of becoming conscious of our daily waste of energy and inherent discomfort, but this does not incorporate ease or comfort into our integrated way of life. We are letting go of muscles whose hypertensions are caused by lack of bone balance and by lack of emotional balance. The fundamental causes must be dealt with if relaxation is to assume its rightful place in the activity of living.

Why is relaxation important? We think of relaxation in terms of our own personal release from strain, but relaxation is a *part of every vital movement of our bodies,* including the action of heart and digestive tract. If we understand its use in our body economy, we will have a better idea of how to attain it. The lack of relaxation is at the root of most chronic ailments.

We rarely think of our behavior in terms of different systems of our bodies. We usually think of our behavior in terms of our own ego consciousness, the "I" behavior, when as a matter of fact our muscles are behaving according to their responsibilities, our bones according to theirs, and each organ with a rhythm of its own.

RELAXATION IS BALANCED ACTIVITY

How does relaxation function in the economy of living? It saves our lives many times a day as we dodge motor vehicles and steer our way through crowded streets. Instead of freezing on the spot in fear, your relaxation mechanism allows your muscles to move your bones safely across the street. When we understand this and get our imagination working on its usefulness, we will not have to "take time off" to attain relaxation. It will become a part of our philosophy of life in our daily thought and behavior.

We become what we think about. We are not what we think we are, but what we are thinking—what we have thought for so long a time that it has entered the unconscious realm of behavior and we are unaware of its existence. These thoughts have been supported by emotions, and may or may not have been initiated in concepts that take place in the cortex or frontal brain. They rarely rise to consciousness. If we learn about relaxation and what it really means, it will become a part of our daily thinking, with resultant outward expression.

Movement is our only means of expression; through movement we evolved. The two phases of movement are extreme activity and complete relaxation. Relaxation is balanced activity reduced to a minimum.

Movement is produced by muscles acting on bones. Tensions are interruptions to movement. When you move, you are moving bones through space. What makes them move? The desired picture of movement in your imagination. What moves the bones? Muscles. How do they move in the precise direction in the exact time needed to follow your picture and with just enough energy (no more, no less) to accomplish your purpose? Your intention prepares deep reflexes over which you have no direct control, except the intention to set your picture of movement in motion. These nerve reflexes have successfully controlled the rhythms of movement throughout the ages for all animals that have survived. They know how to follow the impulses of motion for a life-saving situation. They have continued to function with an intelligence far more fundamental than any direction which you could consciously make to measure a time-space movement. The muscular antagonizers are controlled in the depths of your balanced mechanism, and respond automatically.

The main difference between the response of the animal to movement preparation and that of man is that lying in the imagination of man are many pictures and he can call any of them into consciousness and inhibit the action of any one if he cares to. The decision is his. Thus reconditioning takes place.

If a muscle is relaxed, it can be more readily employed in any form of movement. Its tonicity is balanced. The cat asleep on the hearth catches the mouse that has the temerity to come within its environs. Yet lift the paw of the cat and see what relaxation really is.

The purpose of relaxation is to make movement more efficient in timing and response. When relaxation is considered in terms of letting go, becoming flaccid, the result is interference with both timing and efficiency of the deep inner mechanisms of movement. For relaxation to be valuable and useful, we must understand movement and the role that relaxation plays in the rhythm of all organs and muscles of the human structure. All organs and groups of muscle fibers relax and work alternately in their movement rhythms.

Relaxation is not lifelessness. It is not floppiness of bodily parts. It is *potential activity*. It is only when a muscle loses its tone that it becomes functionless, flaccid, and useless. Relaxation, balanced cellular activity, is potential energy in *abeyance*. This is a positive state, not a negative. When call for quick movement arises there need be no lengthy preparations made to release useless *inhibitions*, neither is it necessary to open closed pathways between generating cells and "sleeping" muscles. The connections are already there. The muscles are in tone and thus in a state of readiness. The time-space-movement mechanism responds on demand.

Neither the wild nor the domestic animal has interfered with his timing system by false education and habits as has man. When needed, the animal's responses come speedily. The need to assemble his living forces touches off his mechanisms.

After completion of activity, he *rests,* more completely relaxed perhaps than man can ever be.

Interpreted as a positive state, as balanced and minimum muscular activity around joints, relaxation points to the need of an intelligent understanding of *the body as a mechanism subject to universal laws.* When its parts are in balance and its various weights adjusted to maintain their positions with the least muscular effort, the body is in equilibrium—at rest. Relaxation is attained!

Unlock your bones and train your emotions through imagination and muscular re-education. Through movement man must learn the meaning of relaxation. The ability to localize movement without introducing tenseness is the mark of a relaxed and balanced body. With balanced tonicity in the muscles, they respond effectively and economically upon call; their fiber bundles make the proper adjustment when needed to establish efficiency in the economy of the whole muscle.

C H A P T E R   I I I

Manifestations of Tension

The manifestations of tension are many. The nervous house-wife and the busy executive show similar emotional and physical symptoms. The face freezes into long lines, its expression vaguely anticipates, not knowing what. The foot taps, the hands fidget, the jaw sets; bodily attitudes stiffen or collapse and breathing is high in the chest. Perhaps liquor, coffee, or cigarettes are added. The eyes are too tired to read and sitting still is a punishment. So the spine slumps, the neck and knees tighten. Interest in diets appears, stimulated by vague internal discomforts.

In many, senses are whipped by fast music or fast motion. At night such persons do not sleep. Their heads swarm with plans and dreams before they drop over the edge toward morning ennui. By day, they become more mechanical in responses or irritable in reactions. Even hysteria may express itself in petty irritations, increasing the tensions through disturbed breathing-rhythms. Such persons are farther and farther away from their own creative levels. They have a growing sensitiveness, and their doubt and instability are the outcroppings of vague fears.

Many of us today are wearied mentally and physically by efforts to cope with the prevailing confusions. On all sides we hear of people who are "too tired to think," "too distraught to focus," "too exhausted to sleep." Under these conditions, the hours of theoretical ease and rehabilitation between sun and sun are usually spent in a stupor of fatigue or at high tension. Admonitions to relax become an irony, and the comfort of real rest seems unattainable.

Everyone has experienced emotional frustrations in one form or another. One can hardly live through a week without being confronted by an emotional crisis. Others besides ourselves may not consider them at all serious, but to us they hold an important place. Perhaps such a crisis arises from a disagreement with your girl friend, your wife, a business associate, or the next-door neighbor. It might be that you are merely angry with yourself for some hasty action. Little matter the cause or how insignificant it appears to others, it bothers you— often to an unreasonable degree. You attempt to think out the proper action to take, how best to remedy the situation, but emotion blurs clear thinking. While you are under this strain, your body undergoes many interesting physiological changes of which you are unaware. The age-old mechanism for meeting emotional crises takes hold and the individual tenses with a varying degree of intensity, depending upon the strength of the emotions experienced. Confusions of this kind are not unusual; we have all faced them.

Tensions result from muscular and structural and chemical imbalance, from emotional disturbances, confused thinking. These are contributed to by lack of oxygen, due to high, shallow breathing produced by the tensions. The resulting toxins in the tissues act as stimulants to muscles already too active. Activity in muscles, with no expansive motion taking place, is a further factor in chemical imbalance. So the high-tension picture increases and becomes a habitual one. Emotional and structural balance *must* be found.

EMOTIONAL AND STRUCTURAL BALANCE

There are two distinct problems confronting the human being in his attempts to live a happy and successful life. The

first is the proper management of the body, the structural units
of which it is comprised—how best to eliminate unnecessary
bodily strains and structural maladjustments. The second is
the psychological problem, the problem of the emotions. We
must acquire a philosophy and have the knowledge with which
to meet any situation in a sensible and straightforward manner.
Emotional and structural tensions are so closely related that
it is often difficult to distinguish between them. Many problems
which seem entirely mental result from physiological causes,
and the reverse is equally true. Static contraction in our surface muscles to accord with pet ideas of personal appearance,
if long continued, reacts unfavorably, not only on bone balance
but also upon the nervous, circulatory, and visceral systems.
There is a loss of mobility at bony articulations. This mobility
is essential for free-functioning muscles. Stiff, jerky joints often
accompany habitual tension.

With poor bone-balance and the muscular strain this en-
tails, efforts are made to seek relief by slumping or by stiffly
"bracing up." Beds, soft mattresses, chairs incorrectly built,
high pillows or no pillows—all make their contribution to man's
tensions. Walking and standing on hard surfaces, riding about
in haste in the midst of gas fumes, make up too large a portion
of civilized life. In addition to all these things come long hours
of work in one position. Many of these handicaps are unavoid-
able, but intelligent adjustments can be made to ease these
strains.

FEAR AND ANGER AS A WAY OF LIFE

The factors contributing to daily tensions are many and
varied—too numerous to list. However, a few of them belong
to everyone's way of life. On the psychological side there are
uncorrected emotional habits. The sensory organism of the
person with an overdose of emotional drive never rests. Such a
person reaches the station before the engine of the train on
which he is riding. One is reminded of the elderly lady from
Cape Cod who was taking her first train ride to New York City.
At every station and between stations, she halted the patient

porter to inquire what progress the train was making. As they were pulling into 125th Street, she grasped his arm on one of his baggage-carrying trips to ask nervously if they were arriving at Grand Central Station. His reply was: "No, ma'am—that's the next station." "Are you sure this train stops there?" she insisted. "I hope to God it does, ma'am! If it don't, you won't live to care!"

Hidden fear and anger appear in various garbs to confuse the emotional balance. From the roots of fear spring anxiety over small daily problems. Undue attention is given to regrets of things past, future troubles are anticipated, and there comes a longing for answers to problems without facing the necessity of finding the answers oneself. Subtly acquiring the reputation of being a very "sensitive" person is a clever and often unconscious way of leading others to make decisions which each should make for himself. There are many other behavior patterns which we can recognize as stemming from the fear root. Guidance missed the mark in babyhood.

Anger, too, can sprout many emotional evils. Being impatient with things and people not conforming to one's particular mental or emotional interests, a form of resentment and egotism, is bred of anger. This evil grows rapidly and causes much unhappiness and tension in oneself and others. Demanding more from the world than one gives is a deep form of resentment; its earlier causes were soon forgotten but it still bears fruit.

Wishful thinking, longing for something to happen that probably never can, is another form of foolish resentment. The results of such childhood habits become real afflictions when life is not full of useful, challenging activity. Intelligent guidance of emotional expression in the early years is needed to prevent childish, emotional imbalances from being carried into adult life.

DELAYS IN THE USE OF SCIENTIFIC KNOWLEDGE

Since the time of the ancient Greeks, there has been a changing style in notions about the position of various parts of the body. Consequently, people have long been "doing things" to "fix" the position of the head, the neck, the shoulders, the hips, the abdomen. The list of posture efforts is long.

Changing styles play no small part in building bodily tensions. The figure of the mannikin in the display window is distorted in its various parts to suit the current style of clothing. This distortioin depends on whether clothing emphasis is placed on the hip, bust, neckline, or the cling or swing of the skirt and its length. The unthinking public tries to imitate it all, believing that one might as well be out of the world as out of style.

For many years man has increased his knowledge of the action of physical forces; he has applied this knowledge to building better and more useful structures. But he has largely failed to apply it to the mechanism which is most vital to him— his own body. Few of us like to face ourselves. We frequently run away from ourselves, seeking release in some extraneous pursuit. This is, to be sure, better than sinking into one's own deep depression. But does it remedy the source of our tensions and maladjustments? Is there anything we can do about it?

The effective use of facts proved by science meets the standardized accepted techniques of a given period and, although these facts may be admitted into our "body of learning" as isolated pieces of added knowledge, organizing them into useful procedures for daily living follows the snail's pace.

The slowness with which the findings of science are incorporated into living is evidenced by the history of the cell theory.

In the seventeenth century, Hooke, a physicist and mathematician, examined a very thin section of cork through a microscope and called the honeycomb arrangement "cells." The cell theory, as a point of view for the study of living organisms, was delayed until Schleiden and Schwann in 1838 threw new light upon the problem. Twenty years later, Virchow advanced the hypothesis that "every animal appears as a sum of vital units, each of which bears in itself the complete characteristics of life." Nearly *one hundred years* elapsed before this information became useful to humanity. It is the basis today of most of our laboratory procedures in biology and biochemistry.

FAITH AND HABIT

Establishing valuable habits is a great time-saving and energy-saving device. You are not safe driving in traffic until the method of driving your new car has become automatic and unconscious. The exact timing of the foot on the brake and the timing of the acceleration determine the exact operation of the car in space; that is, over the road.

Optimistic habits form grooves of behavior. What does this mean? It means that the physical avenue through which the mental and the emotional flow into action are motivated by optimism. The golfer filled with worry does not drive a straight ball. The sprinter who at the moment of preparation doubts his ability falls short of his proved running-time. All champions have experienced the importance of confidence while reaching or trying to reach their goals.

Doubts or fears may come from the tension of indigestion or from emotional dissatisfactions or from various other disturbances. They interfere with movement. The responding mechanisms do not ask where the tensions come from, but their pathways are blocked just the same. These patterns of nerve-muscle response, which carry weight through space in perfect timing and precision, must be free to act unimpeded. Faith and habit operate together in all free accomplishment.

We have faith in the technique of the skill learned. Golf, tennis, swimming, running, jumping, chess, or pool, also mathematical solutions and literary skills. Habits of response have been formed and we have faith in our ability to play the games or solve the problem. When someone offers a different technique for obtaining a better golf score or for the solution of a mathematical problem, we are immediately filled with doubt and hesitation. We must first accept the new technique as a beneficial change over the old. We may then supply it with faith and optimism until it coordinates freely through our body mechanisms. We then repeat this operation until it becomes a habit. So we establish it in our unconscious field of endeavor and find ease and safety in its use. Our adult lives are motivated by habit. Habits may be changed and a greater faith established when more knowledge is obtained concerning any improved method of procedure, either in motor or mental skills.

Man's physical heritage may be observed in the wisdom of the body as seen in the balancing forces within individual systems, biochemical, biophysical, and mechanical. If this physical balance is accomplished by too great an expenditure of energy or too much "backfiring," as when man interferes with this wisdom, the individual is at some point in his thinking either *in ignorance of the facts or in psychological conflict.*

CHAPTER IV

Human Awareness and Reflex Action

Man, who is chemically organized, mechanically balanced, and has a biological foundation, is governed by the individual laws of each of these sciences. Most of these laws govern alike the animate and the inanimate. But man is more. He is ethical, moral, religious. He has reasoning powers. He can choose whether he will be law-abiding or a law unto himself, irrespective of the social order in which he finds himself. Nature, however, he cannot flout! In this respect his limitations are many.

Man's conscious choices make him aware as no other animal is aware. Animals live and breathe and eat, protect themselves from enemies and react in nearly human ways, but they do not realize that they are alive. They do not know that they are aware, although they have awareness. We may say that man is *aware of his awareness.* He can analyze his own consciousness. His self-conscious qualities are not all biological; they include also the chemical and the mechanical.

Superimposed upon the physical and the chemical heritage are the ethical and the rational characteristics of man. But the ethical and the rational are free from the physical and the chemical in the sense that other creatures are physical and chemical, but have not the reason and conscience which abide in man. Man, unlike the animals, can form ideals of justice and truth which serve him in determining his ideas about his behavior and the behavior of his fellows.

Man is subject to physical law but he can make intelligent adjustments according to his knowledge. He can form a philosophy of behavior founded upon psychological findings and he can conserve his energy by becoming better acquainted with known laws of chemistry and mechanics. Man alone is equipped in such a way as to become aware of being aware.

You are doing a great many things at this moment of which you are aware and yet not aware that you are aware. As you now sit reading you may be sitting on a very hard chair, you may be too hot or too cold, the light may be poor, you may be slightly hungry. Of these conditions your many little cell-egos may be aware, as any independent single cell is aware, but until the irritations from stimuli being sent to headquarters become expansive, with more and more cells coming into awareness, the messages they convey escape the consciousness. After you become aware of your awareness, you take appropriate and intelligent measures to correct the situation. You have then become conscious of discomfort, conscious of *awareness*.

A boy sat on the floor reading the comics. A fly persistently wandered across his left eyebrow. He made amusing, almost imperceptible twitches with his left shoulder, and once his hand moved so far as to leave the paper that he was holding down. But not until the fly returned many times and the tickling accumulated enough to overshadow the tickling of his inner risibles did he take appropriate action and "swat the fly." When he became aware of his own awareness his conscious ego dealt with the matter.

DELAYED AWARENESS

Human awareness may be delayed under great emotional excitement, and the muscular activity may be only the *unconscious response* to the needs of the occasion, as is often demonstrated in a fire or a shipwreck. A lineman caught in the tower of a burning building may be unconscious of his broken arm in his effort to escape. Shipwrecked in icy waters, a mother clutching her child may keep afloat for some time, but rescue brings collapse. The boy who came to Napoleon at Ratisbon delivered the message, then fell dead. Your involuntary muscles as well as the voluntary respond under emotion.

CONSTRUCTIVE OR DESTRUCTIVE EVOLUTION

In the unconscious, the emotions, motives, instincts, and memories may mobilize toward the positive, constructive evolution of the individual. Or the reverse may be true. Pessimistic, inhibitory, destructive evolution may likewise organize to retard his progress.

The response to emotion turns in or it turns out. When tensions are the result, they make new impressions on the central neurons (deep nerve cells). Memory records are made of these new patterns which the "I" has not allowed to carry through. The habit of riotous, unguided anger or fear is strengthened, not weakened, by this inhibition.

Thinking may be changed and movement may be commanded, but *emotion cannot be.* Often emotions are concealed even from oneself until they become explosive. Emotions can only be expressed or inhibited. Inhibition is neither commanding nor controlling them.

When we recognize the need for positive expression we reduce our tensions. Tensions are produced by mental fixities and inhibitory emotional habits. These tend to unbalance the natural rhythms of the human body, and thus conflict between the bodily systems may create body poisons. We must become more aware of these imbalances as they occur, so that we may assume intelligent responsibility for them. Investigate the truth about your own reactions. Facts will then replace fancies and constructive action can result.

THOUGHTS AND FEELINGS

Both thoughts and feelings affect our physical mechanisms profoundly. In the imagination you can set up any pattern of movement you wish the body to perform and, with continued attention and desire to move, such patterns are executed. It is thus we learn skills, *all* skills of whatever kind, *mental or physical*. This fact in itself is of major importance, for its use can be of much value to us when understood, and its misuse can affect us to an extent not sufficiently recognized.

An artist may sketch from a model before him, but he can also create a picture of the model or of a daisy field from memory. The architect plans his building, creating it first in his imagination before it takes shape as an actuality. The teacher plans his lesson, the designer his product in the same manner. Naturally, the clearer and more accurate the imagined picture is, the more skillful will be the execution of it. The greater the exactitude and persistence of concentration upon the development and activity of the picture, the better and more efficient will be the movement toward its accomplishment.

Intelligent survival is the result of a type of thinking and doing. Although man has been millions of years developing, he has arrived at the study of how he behaves as he does quite recently; so recently in fact, that he still hesitates to accept the truth when science presents it to him.

SCIENCE AND THE ART OF LIVING

Science and art, although one in life, are separated and analyzed by men of vision for our understanding and use. Science and art act upon all mankind. Through them there is a better understanding among nations. Neither racial nor religious prejudices stand up against them. The laws of the underlying forces of God's operations in the universe are brought to light by inspired thinkers of all nationalities, of all ages!

To the scientist interested in analysis, the human organism may be described in terms of its chemical content and mechanical reactions. His description of the human structure may be as accurate and definite as his description of a rock stratum. But we recognize that the vitality of living must include the emotional reactions as well. The artist translates human structure into thinking, laughing, weeping, adoring men and women.

Both views of structure are important. The scientist's view is analytical, microscopic, detailed—an accurate analysis. The artist and the philosopher combine parts—synthesize the units and give meaning to the whole. For complete understanding of life and its activities both views are essential.

As we study the close interplay between thinking, muscular, glandular, and nervous activities, we find that their smooth functioning depends upon the freedom of action of every little part.

CORRELATION IN BODY SYSTEMS

Many messages must travel over the nerve pathways to central offices to bring about the response which we call living. The receipt of the message and the organization of the responses, whether for inside or outside activity, have been studied as systems by those interested in the determination of body behavior. Through the function of these systems, sensations are carried to centers and motor impulses conveyed from centers to muscles or organs where movement takes place.

There are nine systems controlling the living body: skeletal, muscular, nervous, circulatory, respiratory, excretory, digestive, glandular, and reproductive. How could the cortical brain (frontal), sometimes called the "baby of the brain," being the last to expand and develop, manage the intricate timing mechanism for the conscious coordination of so extensive an army of workers? Our twin coordinators, the conscious and the unconscious, must act together to synchronize the whole! The interrelation of the activities of the systems is called correlation.

Correlation is accomplished in two ways—through changes in movement of body parts in response to mechanical principles, and by organic changes through the response to chemical and glandular action. These interrelated forces are incessantly at work in all types of response in bones, muscles, organs, and nerves. The organic changes come about through the laws governing living tissues, while the mechanical changes result

through the operation of mechanical laws common to all structures.

When we command a movement of arm or leg, we establish all the conditions to effect the movement of several bony
levers in organized action. The wisdom lies not in man's "command" but in the various systems cooperating to establish the
right conditions for body balance. This is effected by coordinated actions automatic in behavior—a whole chain of reflexes!

The multitude of fine adaptations of the body and of its
several parts which enable it to keep a balanced relation with
the forces of gravity and inertia constitute primary patterns
of behavior, and all are dependent upon nervous reflexes.

Reflexes are inherited action patterns. They are automatic
responses to stimulation, able to function at birth. A simple
reflex involves only sensation and response. Throughout the
body an impulse of one kind—sensation—may be translated into
an impulse of another kind—motion—the resulting action being
called a reflex.

Although the mechanism of these simple reflexes is complicated, the responses are so simple they are taken for granted.
Winking, breathing, and the knee jerk lie in this category. These
are protective, instinctive patterns of behavior having no emotional background. They result merely from adjustment to environment. These reflexes are inactive only when there are
organic or functional disturbances in the nervous system.

The *reflex arc* is our nucleus for behavior. This arc includes the stimulus and the response. It forms the so called
"unlearned patterns," the instinctive patterns such as sucking,
breathing, walking. Taken all together, such reflexes constitute
our nervous activity. That which we call consciousness is a great
orchestration of simple reflexes and is too complex for us to
grasp fully. Chains of reflexes, ages old, are so well organized
that their behavior seldom rises to the seat of consciousness.
Most of our movements are affected through them. *In the*

elaboration of the simple reflex mechanism man's learning and conditioning has been made possible. Through purposive movements toward self-preservation, patterns of muscular behavior were developed for his use. Thus survival was possible for both animal and man. Man has inherited these organized patterns and can intelligently make use of them. In his reflexes lie his source of speed and power.

Cellular wisdom resides in the unconscious mechanisms, and in behavior responses its operation is automatic. A simple example of this is the function of breathing. Breathing is partly regulated and operated chemically in the medulla oblongata, the lower part of the brain. Here the blood reports its needs to the sensitive nerve-ends and, together with the action of reflexes whose stimuli are of a mechanical kind, instantaneous response through motor currents to the muscles is effected. We breathe. Even if we willed to stop breathing, the stimuli in the medulla resulting from the chemical necessities of the body would start the diaphragm working. Neither can we prevent the knee jerk when the proper stimulus is given. Much of man's behavior response lies in such types of cellular wisdom.

SENSATION TURNED INTO ACTION

Let us take a simple illustration of the way sensation is turned into action, i.e., the function of the stimulus-response reflex arc. Suppose you touch something hot with your finger. The stimulus occurs at the skin where a nerve end is located. It travels along a sensory nerve to the spinal cord. There it is diverted by an association neuron to a motor neuron, then back to surface muscles which react by pulling away the hand. This may be instantaneous, with little conscious thought given to it.

The stimulus may also travel on through the cord to the brain, where thought occurs, and from the brain it will then descend to the hand for action. Thus choices may be made. One may decide to endure the heat, inhibit the motor nerves preparing for the response, and tense or "freeze" the parts—like the small boy partial to lizards who froze himself in his

seat until playtime to avoid notice by his teacher while he en-
dured the discomfort of a lizard clinging to his bare skin under
his shirt. But much of our action is determined in the spinal
cord. If an emotional "block" is encountered, the stimulus then
must travel to the brain to be interpreted. Thinking is a ready
tool for the emotions. More thinking is necessary when there is
hesitancy or inhibition than when spontaneous action takes
place.

The nerves "play" upon muscles in a continuous stream
of impulses, as an organist plays upon the keys of his instrument. The technique of the musician as to fingering, phrasing,
tempo becomes automatic with practice, but his *control* of the
organ stops always presents the possibility of change in musical
effects.

In man, habit forms definite patterns of muscular coordination in response to nerve stimuli, but there is always the *possibility of creating new stimuli* and effecting new responses
through nerve circuits by more intelligent pictures of organization. That is controlling your "stops" in your mental picture
gallery. As a result the consciousness adjusts itself to new patterns of bodily arrangement and with repetition a new habit is
formed—a *conditioned reflex.* This in time becomes automatic.
All new learnings from babyhood to adulthood follow this
pattern.

THE CONDITIONED REFLEX

Added to the "unlearned patterns," the more complicated
"conditioned reflexes" have developed in the evolution of
man's growth and education. A good football game is the result
of *conditioned reflexes.*

The formation of a conditioned reflex is elemental and
can be comprehended, but its relations are complex and not
easy to trace. They depend upon the internal conditions of the
organism as well as upon conditions of the outer environment.
They are ever changing under repeated experiences. In this
fact lies the hope of overcoming a poor ancestry or strengthening a good one. In this mechanism lies the hope of further

evolution and a higher civilization, the possibility of integration of the spiritual values with factual education. As a man "thinketh in his heart," so he becomes. His emotions and his ideas combine to build his conditioned reflexes and make him what he is.

After the stimuli from the external environment have been received at the surfaces through nerve end-organs in eyes, ears, skin, nose, they are conducted to various central nerve-cells in spinal cord and brain, there to meet conditioning stimuli from within the system. Highly intricate mechanisms integrate and differentiate these stimuli, making ready for the appropriate response. This is a very swift and sure procedure of which we are entirely unconscious until the result of these minute operations rises into consciousness in the form of a desire or a movement. Sensations enter from without, commingle with thoughts and memories from within, also with sensations of fatigue or organic disturbances, and together these stimuli organize our response.

These inherent forces acting upon the substance of an individual organize it in such a way that you are always you and I am always I. Our reactions may be studied and fairly well determined by others observing us because of records made in our sensitive materials of all former reactions. Through these records our habits of thinking and acting have become established and can be recognized.

This is a great energy-saving device when the habits are good. It conserves energy for other purposes. Thinking and organizing have already been accomplished. The very unobtrusiveness of the operation of these mechanisms of stimuli and response, however, blinds us to the effects upon our personality when the habits are less constructive.

THE BRAIN AND ITS RELATION TO CELLULAR WISDOM

The best of man is his inheritance. One should either make the most of it or decide on what he considers the flaws and set about reconditioning the mechanisms of response for better operation, more intelligent expression of unity, wiser social adjustments. Our inherited forces form the reserves in our physical bank-account. Better command of these reserves should be the desire of every one of us.

The nerve centers receiving sensations and initiating motion, coordinating sensations and motions into a complex bodily procedure, are localized in certain masses of cells in the central nervous system.

The brain with its different departments and association fibers, and the two nervous systems which stem from it, are too complicated to analyze here. Through the operation of these many mechanisms, the temporary or learned reflexes (conditioned reflexes), organize slowly into functional systems during the whole of a lifetime. These are the mechanisms which make it possible for us to form new habits or to recondition old ones.

The cerebrum, or frontal brain, is the seat of intellect, of consciousness, reason and imagination, the analyzing power. The cerebellum (behind the frontal) is the seat of coordinating power. These two parts in particular constantly interact; they give birth to the correlation of the stimuli and response system. They establish desired habits by *repeated movement toward their accomplishment, and these in turn establish conditioned reflexes.* The responses then become *automatic!* In these learned reflexes lies the meeting-place of the conscious and the unconscious.

When sensations are accompanied by emotion, the central nervous system mobilizes the individual for appropriate response. All the departments of the brain may automatically function to bring about the desired results. When the faculty of judgment and the power of choice are involved, the intelligence builds upon the instinctive responses residing in the reflexes to express the idea or purpose of the individual. This involves the whole person, the automatic mechanism as well as the conscious command.

Through the cerebral cortex (frontal brain) man chooses behavior desired for objective expression, and through the reflexes the inner man organizes the response in the imagination. He sees it as being done. Thus new habits in thinking and response are slowly formed. New learning is accomplished.

ORGANIZATION AND RESPONSE

The biological forces, through the instinctive patterns, operate as a background for the conditioned reflexes. These have repercussions upon the entire organism. When you have learned to throw a ball, to play golf, or to drive a car, you have turned over your desired technique to the inner man. The avenue of approach is the imagination, and your picturing the movement desired produces the stimuli. The response is accomplished automatically by a series of reflexes.

Impulses may also carry to the viscera (organic content). The systems of reflexes connect with both the viscera and surface skeletal muscles. Vital organs as well as surface muscles respond. If you run too fast you may have palpitation of the heart. If you turn somersaults you may become nauseated. All this reflects the operation of the many reflexes connecting the voluntary and the involuntary systems, the conscious and the unconscious man.

A man who knows what he wants, and would like to get *what he wants when he wants it,* would be interested to find the *throttle of the unconscious,* to know how to turn on the switch between his conscious and unconscious; how to tap that storehouse of energy residing in his unconscious. But he must be content to turn himself over to that smarter man inside —to say "please" and have patience for the response. Imagination and understanding are needed to fulfill these requirements. Man must picture his desired accomplishment and have faith in the bodily response at his command. He is thus a worthy general of his own competent army.

Man's freedom lies in his ability to cooperate intelligently with his inherited behavior. A man can be free only as he releases himself to this deep inner intelligence. At the same time he must have the *faith* that his psychophysical coordina-

tion and equilibrium will carry him safely through. All haz-
ardous techniques such as flying, tightrope walking, racing, are
learned in this way. *An eternal trust is necessary.* Growth in
this faith comes with experience. Optimism results. It must, to
afford success. With the picture of his technique in his imagination, man trusts his inner machinery to function in the time-
honored patterns accurately and precisely. More thinking and
doing, less holding and fixing, is the intelligent way!

The primal urge of all living entities is self-preservation.
The mechanisms successful in survival were obviously the ones
which could adapt to environment, receive stimuli, correlate
them and respond in a way best suited for self-protection. The
stimulus-response mechanism, with its numerous reflexes ready
to function at birth, is man's most valuable heritage.

CHAPTER V

The Living Engine

The acting unit is the muscle. It is an organized unit, a living engine. In it lies the God-given power of life. Without it we could neither express life nor in fact live.

The organized muscle consists of many individual parts— bundles of fibers, connecting tissues, and intermuscular septums (celophane-like partitions between fiber bundles). Every cell of this alert mechanism is supplied with nerves, both sensory and motor. Every cell is supplied also with arterial, venous, and lymph vessels which carry the fuel to be burned, oxygen to make it burn, and are the means of disposing of the waste, the ash resulting from the heat of combustion. A very busy and intelligent engine!

CLOSE ASSOCIATION OF MUSCLES AND NERVOUS SYSTEMS

Muscles are of two kinds. If we use the terms employed by the physiologists to describe them, perhaps their functioning will be better understood. They are the smooth or unstriated, and the skeletal or striated.

The smooth muscles are muscles of our unconscious mechanisms. They maintain the rhythms and functions of organic life. They are the muscles of such vital organs as heart, stomach, and intestines. Their action is slower than that of the skeletal muscles. The two types of muscles are very closely related in their functions through the sympathetic nervous system, that part of the nervous mechanism closely tied in with the emotional demands of the body. It is the contraction of the smooth muscles that produces pallor, blushing, fainting, nausea, and many other disturbing reactions. The action of these smooth muscles is also affected by laughter and joy.

The peculiarity of skeletal or striated muscles is the greater number of stripes or striations contained in their fiber bundles. These muscles act on the bony levers of your body, making possible your conscious, voluntary motions. They are controlled in their action by the *cerebral-spinal* nervous system, sometimes called the voluntary nervous system because it enables us to respond in *desired movements*. Our two nervous systems—the sympathetic or involuntary system, mostly controlling the smooth muscles, and the cerebral-spinal system, controlling the striated muscles, are very closely associated. Through their interrelationship the conscious and the unconscious meet and interact.

STRUCTURE AND WORK OF MUSCLES

It is possible, without going into technical detail, to get some notion of how muscles are constructed. They are made up of many thousands of parallel fibers. Fibers are grouped together into bundles, and bundles of fibers are grouped to form a muscle. Each fiber, each bundle of fibers, each muscle, and each group of muscles is surrounded by a covering of connective tissue and fascia. Nature wisely protects, binds together, and provides continuity throughout the body for the workers of the living engine.

Connective tissues are tough and, in places, thicken to greater toughness—muscles must not break their bounds with our sudden spurts of enthusiasm. A person in ordinary condition, weighing one hundred and fifty pounds, carries around about sixty pounds of meat. Uncooked meat gives us a good idea of the gelatinous consistency of muscles and makes it plain that without bones to support them and keep them in place they would be as impotent as a bowl of blancmange. Muscles are attached to bones at this and that point by their tendons. They are separated from one another by their sheaths, which are also fastened to bone. Thus muscles, their fascia, and the bones form a most complicated mechanism. Bones support weight, muscles act upon bones, and fascia aids to stabilize muscles while acting.

When a fiber of a striped muscle is viewed under the microscope it will be seen to be crossed by alternating light and dark lines, striking in their regularity. It is supposed that hidden under the guise of these stripes lies the machinery for the contraction and relaxation of the voluntary muscles.

The theory of this power of lengthening and shortening harks back to the movements of amoeba-like cells, but it is much too intricate even to sketch here. The contraction is due to rapid nerve-impulses supplied to each muscle fiber. These impulses produce a series of "twitches," succeeding one another so rapidly that they make the muscle fiber tense. When we make a light or feeble use of a muscle, a small number of muscle fibers are contracted, but *always fully so*. More and more muscle fibers come into play as we increase our exertions. As a muscle continues to work, tired fibers drop their work and fresh ones take their place. So the vast hordes of parallel fibers of the voluntary muscles enable us to vary the force of movement and postpone the effects of fatigue, for after a while the power of muscle fibers to contract weakens and finally gives out. Rest and oxygen are needed for recuperation.

An impressive example of what this means is the familiar laboratory experiment of stimulating, by means of an electric current, a muscle removed from the leg of a frog. The contraction of the muscle, which is registered graphically on a moving drum, is sufficient to lift a tiny weight. When the weight begins to drop, if the muscle is at once rested and bathed in salty water, it will come back quickly. It may require five minutes' rest before it can begin to contract again upon stimulus, to lift the weight. If however, instead of stopping the work as soon as there is a reduction in the power of contraction, the muscle is kept under stimulus and made to work longer, the registered curve of contraction will drop quickly until it disappears; that is, until the muscle stops work. Now it will take not five but at least twenty-five minutes to recuperate—an amount of rest equal to the square of the first period. This can be taken as a warning to us in our daily lives. Rest frequently when doing concentrated work, either mental or physical. In both cases your muscles are active.

Owing to the power of muscles to shorten and then loosen, to contract and relax, we can perform the most intricate feats, such as dancing, playing a musical instrument, fencing, or swinging a tennis racket, all of which imply the inerrant and swift contraction and release of great numbers of muscles, large and small. It is impossible to throw just one muscle into action, for even the simplest movement involves the alternate drawing up and letting out of a number of muscles.

PROTECTIVE AGENTS

Accuracy and speed of movement are determined by the *conditioned reflexes and their timing*. They are made safe and sure by the organization and intelligence of the neuromuscular mechanism. Many protective agents lie within the muscles themselves and within the skeletal joints through which movement is possible. The protective agents are so important to the integration of movement of the individual that several examples are cited.

The *two-joint reflex* of the lower extremities dictates the most efficient use of the thighs, knees, and ankle joints. If we do not impose interference, when the thigh is bent the knee and ankle joints *will bend also*. When the thigh is extended, the knee and ankle joints likewise will extend. The former is illustrated in stooping to pick up an object or in landing from a jump; the latter, in rising from the stooping position, or in stepping into an automobile. The two-joint reflex works steadily for us in walking or running.

The *stretch reflex* mechanism serves every skeletal muscle

in the body. It operates thus: when muscle fibers are stretched beyond their easy resting length, they immediately and automatically contract against the stretch. You cannot pull your body asunder. These reflexes not only protect it from possible injury of stretching but they serve many times to aid in movement. The stretch reflex is working *protectively* in the muscles being pulled by the strenuous stretching exercises of the athlete or dancer. He mistakenly thinks he is lengthening his muscle fibers for greater flexibility. But his stretch reflex is working, hindering his movement by shortening protectively the very muscle fibers he is trying so zealously to stretch. When soft tissues are torn during these forced-stretching exercises, the "will" of the worker is being pitted against the automatic function of an inherited, protective mechanism.

The *tensor fascia lata* muscle operates, as its name might imply, to tense the fascia lata, a fascia ensheathing the thigh muscles. As a muscle, it contains relatively little meat; its muscle fibers, however, serve to tighten its sheet of fascia throughout the entire area of the hip and thigh. This fascial sheet spreads to a point below the knee and becomes continuous with the deep fascia of the lower leg. It forms a jacket around the various thigh muscles by connecting with their sheaths and their intermuscular septums. The tightening of the fascia lata prevents any one muscle from overworking to the extent of seriously jeopardizing the safety of the thigh and knee joints.

Most all the deep fascial structures throughout the lower back, pelvis, and thigh are connected and associated in movement with the tensor fascia lata. Because of this, the muscle is sometimes called the posture muscle. Together with the deep pelvic muscles and their fascia, it enables the animal to hold his stance, and man to keep himself erect. It aids in the support of the lower spine, that part of the spine which must lend power to *direction* and *control* of movement. It prevents the individual units of the body from spilling over, as it were, when too much zeal is applied. Undoubtedly this muscle, much more than any other, aids a man in organizing a good swing to carry the ball down the fairway as he develops his golf game.

MAKING MOVEMENTS

What are body movements? Tap your finger on the page of this book, raise your arm, turn your head from side to side. These are body movements, and we rarely ask how we are able to perform them. They seem so simple and yet in reality are mysterious beyond measure. Some would have a ready answer to this question of making movements—we make them with our muscles. This is right, of course, but we may nevertheless forget that without the arrangement of bones and joints no number of muscles could possibly carry out the orders given above. Our common ignorance of our bones is probably exceeded only by our super-ignorance of muscles.

Muscles are the power arms acting on the bones as levers. In organized movement, muscles must move bones away from centers of support and back to center again. Through reciprocal muscle-action this is accomplished. As each bone moves in relation to each other bone, the mean of the distance they move in opposing each other forms an axis. The direction they take is in line with this axis. The speed and direction of the snake moving across the road are determined by this mechanical principle. The bones of his spine are so small that several must be moved in one direction as a segment to oppose other segments. The median line of the power applied is his line of direction, and the distance his segments move away from his median line formed by the curves determines the speed of his movement. The wider the curves laterally, the slower the movement; the more shallow the curves, the faster the movement. Not so much energy is spent in moving weight away from center, so more energy may be used in forward movement.

HOW THE LIVING ENGINE WORKS

Muscles can only *pull;* they *cannot push.* They may seem to push but they can do this only by pulling—that is, by shortening. We think our muscles stick out the tongue or push a door shut or press down a piano key. What we really do is to narrow the tongue by shortening the muscles that run across it. This compression from side to side elongates the tongue. We crook the arm with one set of muscles, and then by straightening it with another set while we have our hand on the door we are able to push the door shut. The bones make this possible. The case of striking the piano key is very similar.

The individual has it within his power physiologically to perform patterns of movement ranging from the fine delicate movements needed in the work of repairing a tiny watch to the highly intricate, complicated movements called for in a ballet dance or in ice skating. Just enough potential energy is stirred into kinetic energy, its working form, to accomplish the act. No waste is evident in the experienced operator. Through intelligent poise, equilibrium, man conserves his reservoir of power and makes his movements sure.

The neuromuscular units, with relaying centers throughout spinal cord and brain, receive stimuli, correlate them, and respond to them. Intelligence should point the way as to how the appropriate response should be made, either mildly or drastically, according to the needs of the situation.

How are muscles able to contract and so pull our bones into various positions? This is still a highly obscure problem. There are very ingenious theories as to the marvels of this unique function. We shall have to satisfy ourselves here with the observable fact that our muscles do shorten to a third, half, or more of their relaxed length, and that as they do this they swell and become firm. By clenching the fist and bending the arm tensely the biceps muscle of the upper arm will shorten and harden. One can see, too, how it lengthens and softens when the arm is relaxed. Each time you try this you will find that you are able to make a better showing than the last time. Within certain limits each repetition brings more fibers into action.

In the muscles lie the rhythms necessary to intelligent living—that is, alternate relaxation and contraction. Good teamwork is expressed in the action of fiber bundles and in the nerve fibers that make this action possible. Since a muscle does not act as a whole, its fibers alternately act and rest as the timing system of the individual requires, in each type of activity. This is another of those invisible, indefinable life-saving devices again demonstrating the wisdom of the body. Here we have another example of the perfect teamwork of the conscious and the unconscious.

PREPARATION FOR MOVEMENT

Researches by physiologists have found that even the smooth muscles form a part of the *preparation for movement* decided upon by the individual. Dr. J. J. R. Macleod has concluded that nerves from the sympathetic nervous system stimulate muscles of blood vessels and respiratory centers and *alter their activity* in preparation for muscular effort.

You decide to throw a ball. That decision comes from your frontal brain. The stimulus from this decision radiates through the motor pathways to the spinal cord and thence to muscles. To quote further from Dr. Macleod: "Simultaneously with the motor action taking place, changes in pulse and respiration are noted in preparation for the desired activity. And this even before there is any time for hormones [products of glands] to be developed, or for reflexes for the muscles that are to operate, to be set up."

If a person expects that great effort will be required for a piece of work, either mental or physical, the pulse and respiration will increase before or simultaneously with the starting of the work, even though it turns out to be a more trivial task than expected. Adequate preparation initiates with expectation! If one's imagination is not factual, if he habitually exaggerates his every problem, he may be flooded with unused energy most of his life.

EXPECTATION CONVERTED INTO PREPARATION

If a muscle is to act to lift a weight, it begins to contract before the load is taken on. The act is automatic in response to expectancy. The stimulus for this takes place in the *thinking process*. This is a prime rule in the conservation of muscular energy.

The nerves initiate movement, the muscles carry it out. It is the nerves that produce the impetus to change potential energy —energy sleeping, ready for use—into kinetic, thus changing the muscle into a working engine. This takes place automatically as the body prepares for the load. To sense this preparation, try, with *fingers relaxed,* to lift a book. Note how heavy it seems and how it almost slips from your grasp. Now put the book down and with a *sense of its weight* grasp it again and feel how light it seems.

Preparations must be made by the body to handle super-imposed weights safely. Our inner mechanisms make this possible. A heavy object, if firm, can be lifted more easily and with greater safety than a light one that is floppy. For example, the muscles can adjust readily to the weight of a board or table, whereas a soft bundle like a bolster or mattress will fall about and have to be caught at *unexpected points by unprepared muscles.* A heavy weight can be received and supported on the foot if it is placed there under control. The tarsus of the foot— the main part of the foot—if balanced and relaxed, will prepare to adjust safely to the load. But dropping a weight unexpectedly on the foot is likely to bring dire consequences and the services of an orthopedic surgeon.

THE SURE EVIDENCE OF THINKING

Muscle response is proof of man's thinking. Man's thinking expresses itself in orderly movement, otherwise we would have no way of knowing that thinking was taking place. When a person gives continuous attention to the solving of a problem, sensitive measuring-instruments would be able to detect muscle changes. The movement of your muscles observed by others, and the fatigue in your muscles as you yourself feel it, are the only bodily proofs we have of thinking. The *product of thinking* as it affects the outside world and yourself is another matter. It has been produced by a vast amount of muscular work and fatigue from activity unseen but none the less real.

Motion is the only real evidence yet discovered that think-ing is taking place. You have no way of convincing others that you have thoughts, feelings, and emotions, except as some movement response conveys a reaction to the observers. It may be but the lifting of an eyebrow or the twitching of the corners of the mouth; but response there must be. If thinking results in inhibition, a slight stiffening of the backbone may be seen by a close observer, also definite changes in breathing rhythms. And if the emotional content in the thinking warrants it, even a pallor or flushing of the face indicates circulatory tensions, for blood vessels as well as bones are moved by muscles. The very thought of arrogance gives an involuntary tip to the head and a protruding chin. The suggestion of inferiority brings a droop to the whole structure. Unnecessary muscular strains are involved in both the Bismarck and the Uriah Heep poses.

WASTEFUL USE OF THE HUMAN ENGINE

When muscles act they move bones. When they grip in fear or anxiety they grip bones. When we grip bones we not only endanger the balance of our finely adjusted mechanical mechanism but also that of our psychic and organic mechanisms. We also interfere with circulation to and from bones.

All the energy expressed in a contracted muscle can be measured in foot pounds in terms of weight displacement. So every static contraction means that each muscle involved is sustaining, in effect, continuously and unnecessarily, an amount of weight directly measurable by the pound pull of its contraction. Everybody knows how wearying it is to carry any weight in the same position for a long distance. Yet many persons in bad posture, through the pull of fixed contractions, carry the equivalent of several pounds suspended by one muscle group for days or weeks at a time.

For example, static contractions in neck, shoulder, and chest muscles persist over long periods of time. They seldom completely release, even in sleep. As these muscles maintain static contraction (tension), they not only hold the weight of shoulders and ribs higher on the spinal column than their bony attachments to the spine require, but they interfere with the balance and free movement of the spine itself, as well as the freedom of circulation to the head. Static contractions register in the central nervous system as sensations of discomfort, but too frequently they are unrecognized as contractions until discomforts turn into pain and pain becomes persistent.

ECONOMY IN THE WORKING UNIT

The muscular system is so well arranged that your desired movements can be carried out with unconscious but precise control. You can loosen the seeds from a grape with your tongue although you may have no idea what muscles are involved or how they work. A surgeon who removes a cataract from an eye might have difficulty in describing to you the muscles he used in performing this operation or how he used them. Yet he may employ much or little force, be accurate in timing, and precise in the amount of force used.

Reciprocal muscle-action, through the stimulus-response system, automatically maintains balanced movement of the bony levers. For example, if you brush a fly from your forehead, the muscles on the outside of your arm must *release their control* at the same time the muscles on the inside *contract* to move the arm through space, with tempo speeded up or retarded according to the emotional drive behind the idea. If the fly happens to be a mosquito, increase of speed and energy applied may easily be imagined. Reciprocal muscle-action implies muscular release on one side of a bone and contraction on the other to enable a bone to move through space.

CHAPTER VI

Nature's Mechanical Triumph

The skeleton is nature's mechanical triumph. Lines of force go through its bones, and the feeling of motion is in them. The living machine walks! Life and death are the extremes of meaning in bones. The skeleton clanks in the ghost history, in the fraternity initiation, and the advertisement. Literary and religious imagery make this most enduring part of the body stand for all of it. The singer of "weary bones" suggests that the very essence of man is tired.

Shakespeare felt bones. In his epitaph they are the last stand of personality—"Cursed be he who moves my bones." In Macbeth, bones are obversely a symbol—"Thy bones are marrowless, thy head is cold." Most of us live a long life with only fragments of feeling and thought about bones. Our bones, more than two hundred in number, have names hard to remember. Why try?

Ignorance of qualities of bone is as great as that of names of bones. Qualities are important. Elementary chemistry-experiments with bone show that acid softens it, but fire burns it to a crisp. A child's bones are soft as gristle; an old man's bones are brittle and break easily. Broken bones are painful, but living bones mobilize to heal and repair their injured or infected parts. Their blood cells hastily devour enemies and marshal all forces for complete recuperation. These things represent important life-giving qualities in bones.

The intelligent person realizes the skeleton inside his entire body is alive and active. In this sense a daring anatomist was modern four hundred years ago. Versalius, who died in the year Shakespeare was born, drew a skeleton which might be a Hamlet standing by a library table, weight on one leg, left elbow on the table. The figure leans forward a little, hand on cheek. The rock, shrubs and leaves at the feet suggest the unfolding of nature's science. The student's pose at the table looks toward the invisible universe of philosophy. The skeleton lives, stands. In a moment it will turn, walk, move body, head, and hand in the soliloquy. It is impossible not to feel that this skeleton lives!

LIVING BONES

The bony framework is separated from the rest of the body for study, but we must think bones *alive* if we are to understand the interdependence of them and the adjoining soft tissues. They work for us and we can improve their service by understanding how their work is best accomplished.

In common with other tissues of the human body, bone has the recuperative quality which is the unique property of all living substance. Bone repairs itself after injury, although at a slower rate than that of other tissues. Bones are ruddy with life currents. They are chemically and mechanically responsive to bodily needs. Mechanically, bones carry our weight, *and should be allowed to do so.* Chemically, they not only repair their own living tissue, but they aid in repairing other body tissues by manufacturing red blood cells to feed all brother cells. Without their manufacturing marrow, other tissues could not live. Bone cells have the ability to multiply rapidly, to organize their materials, to shape their materials so that a long bone shall be made for the leg and a short one for the small parts of the fingers.

The cells which are the bone-fiber builders assemble the mineral matter which insures the hardness and strength of the bone, building the walls of their cells with lime salts. These cells are called osteoblasts. Throughout the years of growth of the bone they continually shape it to meet the body needs. The meshwork of flexible, living fiber must be filled and stiffened by deposits of mineral salts to function mechanically as a weight-bearing framework. Bone must have strength for endurance, firmness to resist compression, and a degree of yielding to sustain shock.

Growth of bone takes place, not as one might suppose, on the ends where there are constant weight and movement disturbances, but at both ends of the midsection. During the time of growth, when bones are constantly altering and rebuilding, they never lose their design. This tenacity of design survives all normal growth and change.

BONE AS A VASCULAR ORGAN

Throughout bone, lengthwise pathways mark the blood supply. These pathways are connected by many cross-pathways whereby blood can bring nourishment to the inside of bones and to tissue covering bones. The adhering covering tissue, the periosteum, is in turn a supporting bed for the blood vessels and nerves going to and from the bone. Periosteum also offers anchorage for tendons of muscles. In the fine meshwork of bone cells and in the covering of bones is a consistent awareness which understands the needs and uses of its own particular mechanism.

Red blood cells are manufactured within the marrow of bones. This marrow fills the canal-like space within the bone shaft. When we realize that the life span of a red blood cell is only about ten days and that the number of red cells in the bloodstream is computed in millions, the degree of activity in bone marrow becomes astounding. Bone marrow prepares for another duty toward the end of its bone shaft—it becomes spongy, that is, cancellous. This cushions the bones from shock and aids in the support and carrying of weight. At the upper end of the thigh bone, the longest, largest and strongest bone in the body, the arrangement of the cancellous tissue is remarkable. It has an intricate, lacy design within the bone, very tough but flexible. Kick a football and you will realize that the thigh must be able to bear much weight and absorb many shocks.

The long bones are especially full of life and activity. It is in the marrow of the long bones that the factory for the red corpuscles, the tiny blood cells, exists. These red cells carry oxygen throughout our bloodstream. If we suffer from a hemorrhage the factories must speed production to meet the need. Arteries and veins run in and out of little holes in the bones. This in itself is a very important reason for *reducing* the grip on bones of habitually tense muscles. Soften this grip frequently.

MECHANICAL INFLUENCES

In their mechanical capacity, bones serve as our framework for support and for the protection of our vital organs, blood vessels, and two nervous systems. The most important mechanical function of bones is to endure pressure stresses. Their cells and fibers seem to be arranged to meet compression (pressure) stresses more successfully than those stresses caused by tension (pulling).

It is generally known that bone fractures always start on the side where pulling stresses occur; not on the side of pressure stresses. This seems to indicate that bones are best adjusted for the bearing of weight. Bone is provided with a material which yields to weight and pressure without breaking or bending, and is capable of making speedy adjustments in its cellular arrangement to superimposed weight. This response of the bone to pressure is of special interest to us in the study of the balance of bones in the human structure.

As we know that bones are sensitive and yielding, it is clear that poor body balance causes disturbance in the bone substance itself. This far-reaching principle, stated by Julius Wolff in 1868, has become known as Wolff's Law: "Every change in the form and the function of bones, or in their function alone, is followed by certain definite changes in their internal architecture, and equally definite changes in their external conformation, in accordance with mathematical laws."

If you were to saw a long bone lengthwise, you would find that it appears hollow throughout much of its length. You would find also that its intricate cellular arrangement resembles patterns of construction which modern engineers have found to combine at once the greatest strength with lightness. It suggests the arch of a bridge or railway trestle. Its long fibers run in parallel columns, crossed by a series of transverse fibers and connected in such a way as to fashion a firm supporting tissue. This is shaped in a fine lacework of bony braces. The result of this design is elasticity, and it offers the greatest mechanical advantage to sustain weight compression.

This mechanical advantage within the individual bone is supplemented when bones are laced together in parallel position. An example of this is seen in the lower leg, where a slender bone, the fibula, is attached to the shinbone, the tibia, by an interlacing membrane. This lacing is called interossecus ("between bone") membrane. It resembles the structure of a snowshoe, adding lightness and elasticity to the weight-supporting strength of the bones of the lower leg. The tibia bears the body weight and the fibula is laced to it for strength and flexibility, but bears no weight directly itself. If it were not for such a snowshoe lacing of these long bones, the size and weight of one bone sufficiently strong to carry and move the weight of our bodies would be impossibly cumbersome. This device is also one of nature's methods of shock absorption. The interlacing tissue allows slight movement between the bones, so that the chance of breaking your leg when you slip on a banana peel is negligible.

Intelligence resides in bone cells. Awareness of conditions and the ability to meet them resides in bones. Thus, through the structure and arrangement of their framework, bones meet successfully these essentials for support, balance, and movement of the body: stability, flexibility, and ability to absorb shock.

SYNCHRONIZATION

When we walk across the floor, muscles are intelligently moving the bony levers in opposing directions to effect the organized rhythm of movement. This makes an *axis of direction in movement*. This axis is formed by the changing opposite positions of all moving parts. The central reflexes control the neuromuscular units which act on the bones to move them in opposition to each other in time-space arrangements according to the laws of motion. We may command movement but we do not command muscles. They operate through our age-old reflexes. Body rhythms are too intricate to trust them to our limited judgment.

When we command movement of arms and legs we expect organized response. The wisdom for this operation lies in the reflexes and the neuromuscular mechanism. When right conditions are established all forces, mechanical and biological, behave according to the laws governing them. As muscle power is applied to the bony levers, accurate movement takes place, bones and their muscular attachments being so arranged as to give direction and mechanical organization to movement.

As a hunter sights a deer, many systems must coordinate with exactitude. The measuring of space, holding a stance to prepare for the recoil of the gun, steadiness of nerve and purpose—all this and more must be in perfect timing. When a man aims a gun a whole chain of reflexes is in process of synchronization. These reflexes are *preparing* as he decides what he is going to shoot. He gets his stance, adjusts his shoulder and spine to the weight of the gun, projects his eyes in aiming, establishes a deep physical quiet and changes breathing rhythms. Many conditioned reflexes effect this, and act to manage his weight and the weight of the gun, keep his eye distance correct, and his head balanced to insure his stance. He must absorb the recoil from the gun in his backbone and legs.

A man's deer- or duck-shooting skill depends upon chemical, mechanical, and organic functioning—automatic in response when conditions are right. With optimism, in a body well-conditioned, unhampered by doubts and fears, his game is assured. His responses result from given conditions. When he has the feeling that "all is ready," it happens, exactly as "it snows, it rains" because *conditions are right*.

Muscles apply power to move the various bony levers and

thus move in a precise direction the weight they carry, each bone or group of bones opposing the other in perfect timing. This response follows the mentally designed movement, the picture in the imagination. And this through the ramification of the intricate nervous system which calls into play all the reflexes!

BONES PROTECTIVE TO VITAL SYSTEMS

Vital systems are housed within and protected by two well-built bony canals. These two canals lie parallel to each other and are in a vertical position.

The housing of the posterior canal includes the skull and the deep portion of the spinal column. In this canal lie the brain and the spinal cord.

The housing of the anterior canal includes the spine, ribs, and pelvic bones, completed at the front by the inner abdominal wall. Within it lie the vital organs of the body, such as lungs, heart, large blood- and lymph-vessels, liver, stomach, and organs below. The bones of both canals are tied together and reinforced by strong ligaments. Through the organisms residing within these two vertical canals all the many systems of the body are maintained, motivated, and recuperated for the activities of living.

Along the spinal column on each side, within the visceral canal, lies the ganglionic portion of the nervous system, often called the sympathetic nervous system. This part maintains the strongest associations between all systems of the body, as it has been the longest in evolution. This system together with the spinal cord effects communication between the body and the brain. Along the front aspect of the spine, also within the visceral canal, lie the largest tubular structures of the circulation, respiration, and digestion. Their systems constitute the vital supply of your body.

Although the spinal column is an important protective center, it is also a coordinating center for both structural and organic rhythm. It is the center from which all muscular and supporting power must stem.

So we find that our bones support weight, reinforced by fascia and ligaments, manufacture red blood cells in their marrow, and protect the many systems contributing to vitalized living. Your bones play a large part in your sense of control and position in your world. The way you balance and use them determines your degree of self-possession and command of your forces.

Common Denominators of All Structures

All substance yields—the glass to the wine, the desk to the writer, and the locomotive to the hurricane. All substance is in a condition of resistance, technically called stress. Stress always tends to cause departure from alignment, especially in an upright.

Pull rubber and it yields, pull wood and it yields, pull steel and it yields. But structural steel yields only after four times as much pressure or pull as that required to break wood. A fifty-foot steel rod in a vise which pulls both ways may stretch ten feet before its molecules separate and give way. It is interesting to note that when this happens, if the force has been applied gradually under control, the break is not a jagged one, but the broken ends follow the pattern of its molecular cohesion, resembling somewhat the smooth ends of a pestle and mortar. If, on the other hand, steel is still warm after casting, it will stretch like molasses candy. Steel is the strongest of the building materials because of this great elasticity. It successfully resists all small stresses.

The more elastic a substance, the more quickly it returns to its original size and shape after a stress has been applied to it. If you ask someone to name the most elastic substance he knows, more often than not the answer will be "rubber." This idea is a popular misconception. We speak of a rubber band as an "elastic band," but such is not the case. Rubber, quite the contrary, is one of the most inelastic of substances. Its usefulness depends upon its ability to transform the energy of a stress (whack of bump) into heat, without injury to a structure. Feel an automobile tire after it has been run for a distance, and see how hot it is. Draw a rubber band between the closed lips several times, and notice the heat produced by this action. Measure a piece of rubber before and after stretching and you will find that it has increased in length; it has not returned to its original size and shape.

One of the more common elastic substances is ivory. Billiard balls, which must impart their motion to other balls without appreciable loss of energy, are made of ivory. Quartz, too, is almost perfectly elastic. Its molecular formation makes it so. Bone is also elastic. It must be to resist stresses successfully in a dynamic being. Bone is more like ivory than any other of the elastic substances. Both are *living products*—they have been developed by living protoplasm.

SIMILARITIES IN ANIMATE AND INANIMATE

All forces in the universe operate in precise ways in similar mechanisms. The human mechanism, being the masterpiece of God's handiwork, duplicates every architectural design possible to the imagination of man. Our study for the better management of man's physical being is therefore to find the patterns and to interpret the forces in man's mechanical structure. The difference between living and nonliving matter is not so great as we might suppose. There are many common denominators.

In the physical universe there are certain principles underlying the action of both the animate and the inanimate. Pressure changes, gravitational changes, chemical, temperature and radioactive changes take place alike in man, the tree, the bridge, and the skyscraper.

The forces of the common denominators are basic to the biological forces, that is, the biological forces in the evolution of living creatures were inevitably obliged to work with the *already established universal laws.* Otherwise, the cellular structure of the animal would be under special dispensation in the arrangement of the cosmos and would need to have no obedience to the laws of the solar universe. But the proof of this need is convincing when we try to live unaided at the bottom of the sea, or thirty thousand feet in the air.

Man erects a building that rests in one place. Nature produces a living organism that is capable of swift and varied movement. She finally tips this structure up on its beam-end after thousands of years of being adjusted to a four-legged position and, with varied success, makes it walk on two legs. This is no valid reason, however, for man to fail to meet intelligently and efficiently the cosmic forces.

GOOD ENGINEERING

When an engineer is given a problem of construction he must consider the substances to be used in relation to the forces which will act upon them. He must picture their best arrangement to meet all possible strains. The effective arrangement of the human structure follows similar engineering principles. Structure in man relates to function in precisely the same way that it does in buildings. It is susceptible to forces that tend to tear it apart and, in the final analysis, is an expression of the forces that play upon it.

The fundamental difference between substances which are used in artificial structures and the substances we find in the human body is, of course, the power which resides in all living cells to reproduce, to recuperate, to repair, and to initiate activity. An outstanding peculiarity of living substance is its metabolic function—the constant alteration of its cells, the giving off of waste products, the accepting and assimilating of new material for its recuperation, and its ability to respond in the fulfillment of man's wishes.

THE INTERPLAY OF FORCES

In the universe all objects are the synthesis of external and internal forces. These forces organize and maintain the general configurations which make animate as well as inanimate objects recognizable and familiar. The stars of a specific constellation appear in a certain relation to one another; a tree, a leaf, a house, even a cloud during its brief moment of visibility—each may appear as a fixed shape. Yet the fixity of shape and identity exists only by virtue of a *great flux and flow* of forces and their balancing action. Moreover, within each general configuration, no matter how fixed it may appear to us, there is a *movement of parts* in constant adjustment and readjustment. Many of the adjustments achieved by man in combinations of structural materials are copies of nature's successes.

Man in his own organism illustrates design maintained by the balance of forces. Nothing in architecture goes beyond nature's achievements in functional design.

Any substance—stone, steel, timber, concrete, muscular tissue, or bone—maintaining balance between two opposite forces or sets of forces is in a condition of what engineers call stress. These principles of balance apply equally to the human and to the inanimate structure. They must be understood in order to interpret the origin of stresses which the human structure is continually called upon to meet.

Man's inner forces—intellectual, social, emotional, and motor—flowing from the human reservoir through bodily mechanisms, must meet the cosmic forces, such as gravity, atmospheric pressure, temperature changes, radioactive forces, and strike a balance with them. These cosmic forces act upon human beings as they act upon Rockefeller Center and the George Washington Bridge, and must be considered when better balance of the whole physiological content of man is to be studied.

GRAVITY AND ITS INFLUENCE

The human body, the bridge, and the tree are all alike in being constantly called upon to struggle for balance between an unceasing attack and an equally unceasing defense of gravity. The defense is that *resistance to penetration* with which nature has in some degree endowed the whole earth, both land and water. Equilibrium of the bridge, building, tree, or human body, a condition of nondisappearance as a whole toward the center of the earth through the pull of gravity, must be supplemented by a condition of similar balance of each part of the structure, and even each particle of the structure with respect to its neighbors. Molecular and cellular balances must accompany mass balance.

The downward pull of gravity on the twentieth floor is in balance with the upward push of the supporting columns of the story below, just as the total pull of gravity on the building *as a whole* is in balance with the upward resistance or push of the *ground under its foundations.*

The downward pull of gravity on the human head is in balance with the upward push at the top of the spine, just as the total pull of gravity on the body as a whole is in balance with the upward push of the floor or the ground beneath our feet. Each structure as a whole, and each part of a structure, is thus in a condition of equilibrium between contending, opposing forces. *There can be no force without its opposite.* Force does not exist by itself; it is a symbol of acceleration. Through it, forms and changes evolve. Every structure is a force diagram. There is a diagram of force in any tangible substance—the atom, the molecule, the cell. The bony framework of our bodies is a design of forces seeking balance.

RESULTANTS IN OPPOSING FORCES

In organized movement in the human being opposition of parts is necessary. Forces acting about the axes of direction formed by the movement of the opposing parts must keep the weights controlled within the middle third of contacting bony parts and of the base of the structure as a whole. A mass loses its balance when its center of gravity falls outside the middle third of its base.

An axis is the resultant of opposing forces in the moving units. These axes must so organize as to keep the equilibrium of the mass of the whole and give direction to movement of the parts. The moving structure must be able to regain equilibrium after expanded movement takes place.

One of the essentials for the stability of a structure is that the axis passing through the center of gravity of the mass must fall within the middle third of the base. To exemplify the "middle third" we may picture that an axis falling through the center of the Leaning Tower of Pisa would fall within the middle third of its base yet it would not fall within the center of its perpendicular mass at all levels. An earthquake could shift its vertical axis just far enough outside the middle third to make its balance insecure. If and when this should happen, the Leaning Tower of Pisa would be doomed.

Many have observed in others or experienced in themselves this tottering on the verge of the middle third, hoping to be able to swing the body weights back to center before the final fall.

Whether weights are balanced sitting or hanging, their forces still operate around an axis. A swinging pendulum passes its axial point with every swing. Its forces are balanced around its axis. A picture hanging on the wall, or your arm hanging in relaxed position from the shoulder girdle, is less dynamic than the pendulum, but its forces of weight are still balanced around its central axis if it falls directly under its support.

EARLY IDEAS OF STRUCTURE

From the day of Archimedes, whenever a man guessed something about structure, he tried it out. The simplest bridge —the log thrown across the brook—has a mechanical principle, a mathematical solution. The wooden suspension bridge, supported by straps of hide fastened to the trees on shore, hung over water in early China, Japan, India, Tibet, and Mexico. The builders obviously managed successfully the problems of bending, shear, and torsion. The first structural guess may have been inspired by some deep part of man's own body.

BRIDGES

The whole problem of balance of forces in movement appears clearly in the long bridge. The first wire suspension bridge in this country capable of bearing a train and locomotive was built across the Niagara River by John Roebling, who was called "man of iron." He had seen a suspension bridge held by chains and he began working on a plan based on wire rope. Previously, he had built a suspension bridge across the Mononga-hela at Pittsburgh. Upon finishing it, he said, "Wind has no effect. When a heavy truck passes across a span, the adjoining pendulums move one half inch. By this accommodation of the pendulums all jarring of the cast iron towers is avoided. The pendulums direct the resultant of any forces . . . through the center of the towers, as well as of the masonry below."

A few years later he submitted plans for the Niagara Sus-pension Bridge. He said of this, "The strength of the cables I have based on the weight of the locomotive and train—245 tons (vertical impact at twenty miles per hour—400 tons), the weight of several teams likely to be on the bridge at the same time and the weight of a foot of snow which might fall. Add five times the strength of wire which would support the tension for these pressures and we will be on the safe side."

The skeptics on this project were silenced when they heard Roebling offer to give financial security for the complete success of the whole and all its parts. When the bridge was taken down forty-two years later, the wire rope still retained its elasticity. He accomplished the intricate problem of engineering success-fully through mathematics and known laws.

Roebling's son, as chief engineer of the Brooklyn Bridge, personally superintended the setting of the caisson foundations for its towers. A caisson is a box of timber, open at the bottom, which rests on the river bed ninety feet below high water. These caissons serve as the "feet" of the bridge. The bridge of 1883 looks as modern today as Rockefeller Center. In a biography of the Roeblings, Hamilton Schuyler calls attention to the careful calculation of opposition of upward and downward thrust and the mathematical meaning of so many thousand pounds load demonstrated by these great bridge-builders.

The pneumatic caissons of the towers and the steel-chain ties procured for the bridge a mobility which made it possible for enormous unequal weights to enter at one end and be safely carried across a movable structure to the other end, and so to terra firma. Sixty-five years' service, and the strength of youth still in its "sinews"! All made possible by a mathematical balance of forces holding structural form to function!

SKYSCRAPERS

Louis Sullivan said that before he was eight years old he had built a dam and had been thrilled at the sight of a suspension bridge. Interest in buildings did not appear until he was twelve. Sullivan lived to be called "master," and to originate the American skyscraper.

A skyscraper is a steel bridge standing on end, with passenger cars running up and down it. The steel of the skyscraper has supplanted the outmoded architectural theory that a building should have three parts—base, shaft, and crown. Chiefly, the skyscraper has verticality and is called "functional." It has foundation—"feet"—a vertical strut, and horizontal fill; no ornamentation. Without steel it never could have been developed.

A tall structure upon a narrow base must support its load through materials having *elasticity added to the qualities of hardness and stiffness.* Steel is the only known substance which could successfully meet the forces acting upon Rockefeller Center or the Empire State Building.

The Neoclassic, Renaissance, and Romanesque style-adaptation have given way before the structural logic of steel. Grain elevators, radio towers, masts, silos, factories, steamers, racing cars, and airplane hangars follow the straight line. Just as the skyscraper depended upon the advent of steel, so the security of man's erect structure depended upon the evolution of bones.

OPPOSITION OF PARTS IN STRUCTURES

Given the steel skeleton of today, how does the architect plan to resist the forces which would cause the parts of the building to slide or twist in one direction or another? He does this by supplying their opposites. How this works is told implicitly in the story of an extraordinary case, the erection of the Imperial Hotel in Tokyo.

When a boy, the architect Frank Lloyd Wright had witnessed the collapse of a building in which the contractor had cheated in meeting the compression stress. He had filled with rubble great piers that were specified to be solid concrete. The architect's terrible responsibility for human life in structures carrying weight shocked and impressed the boy.

When planning the Imperial Hotel in Tokyo, Mr. Wright said, "I studied the temblor, found it a wave movement of earth accompanied by terrific shocks no rigidity could withstand—long piles would oscillate and shake the structure—the foundation should be short or shallow . . . eight feet of surface soil and sixty to seventy feet of soft mud were below. That mud seemed a cushion to relieve shocks . . . why not float the building upon it? Why not a building made as the two hands thrust together, palms inward, fingers interlocking—a flexure, flexing and reflexing in any direction—why fight the quake?"

Like the interlocking fingers which gave Mr. Wright the idea of shock absorption in his inanimate structure, the radial muscles and fascial structures of our framework interlock on the upright supporting spine, and thus direct and redirect movement and absorb shocks through the rocking pelvis as it rests on the movable legs.

To return to Mr. Wright: "How to make the flexible structure instead of the foolish, rigid one. Divide the building into parts. Where parts are more than sixty feet, join these parts and manage the joints in the design. Why not carry the floors as a waiter carried his trays? Supports centered under floor slabs, instead of resting floor slabs on the walls at their edges. That means the cantilever. The cantilever is the most romantic —most free—of all principles of construction." (Our bony pelvis is a cantilever structure.)

The walls of the Imperial Hotel grew thinner as they neared the top, the whole structure was a double shell with piping and wiring free of the main construction. Thus the project of a mighty adaptation of local style, climate, material, labor, and needs, made in the desire to help Japan make the transition from wood to masonry! As the construction was nearing completion, an earthquake shook it. The architect was knocked to the floor. He said, "As I lay there I could clearly see the ground swell pass through the construction above. No deviation appeared in the foundation levels." After the great quake of 1923 the eighty-year-old Baron Okura, who had backed the originality of the architect against Japanese opposition, cabled, "Hotel stands undamaged."

MECHANICAL STRESSES

The complicated science of static engineering is built upon a mathematical determination of an equality of forces acting upon any body so that the resultant shall produce stability with the least amount of strain within the structure. Pressure downward upon an object must be equalized by an upward thrust; forces pulling in one direction must be resisted by equal forces pulling in the opposite direction; forces twisting in one direction must be counteracted by equal forces twisting in the other direction; forces causing one part of the structure to slide upon another must be resisted by equal forces to keep it from sliding.

The engineer names four stresses: axial, shearing, bending, and torsion. Axial stresses, the most favorable of the stresses, include tension and compression—that is, lengthening and shortening. These two stresses travel along the axis, hence the name, "axial stresses." Bending, a combination of unbalanced tension and compression, is the most dangerous of all the stresses. It disconnects the existing axis and compensations must be made. Eventually it may include the imbalance produced by all the five possible stresses. Bending is often called the "sin of unequal resistance." It places any structure at a disadvantage for supporting weight.

In order to maintain its equilibrium, the human body must be in balance with all forces acting upon it. Engineers are able to predict with mathematical precision what to expect of their projects under given conditions. We cannot, however, yet apply mathematical formulae to the stresses produced in the human body by the forces acting upon it. Nevertheless they are important and can be successfully regulated.

Beware of using any portion of the spine as a hinge joint for bending. Bend the head at the top of the spine; bend the trunk at the thigh joints. When more bending is needed distribute it throughout the spine, not at one spot or one region of the spine; bend the spine in a universal curve.

HUMAN BRIDGES

In the human structure we have two bridges with the weight entering at one end and being delivered at the other. In both bridges all movable parts so adjust to the load that the weight is carried safely across. These two bridges are the bony pelvis and the foot.

Weight from the upright spine passes to the pelvic base *at the back*, is carried through the mobile pelvic bony structure to the rotary joints of the thigh at the front. Weight then passes through the thigh, the knee joint, and the lower leg to fall upon another "bridge," the *tarsus* of the foot—the longitudinal arch. Thence it passes to the anterior part of the foot, where quick adjustments by many small parts are made to receive it and to counter its thrusts.

The two bridges, the pelvis and the foot, should always have their tensile members, in other words ligaments and muscles, free and in good working order for service. Upon them depends the tensile strength of the bridges. They correspond to the steel chains of the Brooklyn Bridge, in which the tension forces balance the compression forces with mathematical precision. The pull of the chains balances the weight passing down through the pillars.

All objects operating under applied energy—steam, electricity, or nerve power—are in dynamic balance. Asleep or awake, man is in dynamic balance. But he may be in an economic or in a very expensive balance. This depends on how closely his biologic forces cooperate with the cosmic forces lying in the common denominators. The more human energy

The Two Bridges of the Human Body

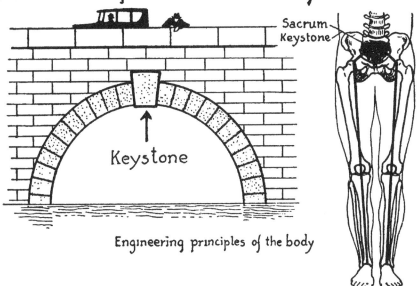

Keystone

Sacrum Keystone

Engineering principles of the body

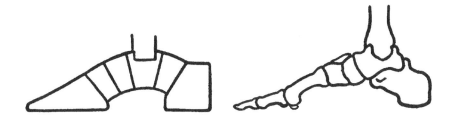

he must generate to hold in adjustment his various parts—bones —the less he has for the work in hand. Intelligence should lead him to find the least expensive way to adjust the numerous parts of his body in relation to the various forces acting upon it.

CHAPTER VIII

Time and Space

It is difficult for us to get the feeling of the speed of our revolving earth, the speed of light, sound, and other forces playing through objects in our physical environment. Many of nature's operations are hidden to our senses, yet unseen forces are an important part of the composite of our lives. Every force changes in relation to the action of other forces upon it. You and your controls represent these forces in operation. These opposing forces maintain your organic, chemical, and structural balances.

A bow and arrow lying upon the table offer no problem in activity. There is a balance of forces in all three—the table, the bow, and the arrow—all quiet and serene, at rest. Lift the bow to the shoulder and place the arrow against the string. We see no change in the table, in the bow, or in the arrow, although we know there is a change in the molecules of each. When, however, your power is applied to the taut string and we see the propelling force of its release in the flight of the arrow, we realize fully that movement is taking place; energy has been expended, new balances are being sought.

Potential energy, in the archer, the bow, and the arrow has released its force into work, the kinetic form of energy. An object is changing its position in space. It travels on momentum. This varies according to the number of other forces acting upon it, such as the power of the wind, the height of the arrow. When momentum becomes weaker than other forces acting upon it, the arrow responds to gravity, falls to earth, and seeks new balances. Horizontal forces have given way to vertical forces. As soon as all opposing forces acting upon it are again balanced—equal and opposite—it appears to our senses inactive, quiet, at rest. And yet we know that this is not true. Its opposing forces are maintaining balance, but they are active, struggling to keep their equilibrium in a fast-moving world.

UNSEEN FORCES

Many important discoveries of today acquaint us with these unseen forces which our senses fail to register, but which science is proving to be the most important factors in life today. In the color spectrum we have infrared and ultraviolet, those vibrations of light outside the range of the human eye. We have infrasonic and ultrasonic in the auditory field, those vibrations of sound outside the range of the human ear. These light and sound waves are so important, however, that they may be found capable of either increasing life or destroying it. The therapy of light and sound offers hope for the future. In the unseen we find our greatest forces of life.

Huxley was saying in 1893, "The more we learn of the nature of things, the more evident it is that what we call rest is only unperceived activity; that seeming peace is silent, but strenuous battle . . . it [the cosmos] assumes the aspect not so much of a permanent entity as of a changeful process, in which naught endures save the show of energy and the rational order which pervades it."

That which we call material is in reality bombarding impulses of energy seeking and attaining balance. It is difficult for us to realize either this great activity or the tremendous power lying in these unseen forces.

Time is the essence of motion. Our perceptions are not keen enough to follow the velocities even in our own behavior; our reflexes must operate in that essence. Einstein's fourth dimension is experienced without recognition by our sensory organism but, analyzed, we may get a feeling for it.

The following is of interest to note. Said Nunn in 1923 in the London Press: "Like many other great scientific ideas, the Principle of Relativity, with which the name of Albert Einstein is imperishably associated, is rooted in observations familiar to everyone. Those most germane to our purpose are simple observations concerning motion. Most of us have from a pier-head watched a steamer cast off and quietly recede; and at another time, being ourselves on board, have had the queer experience of seeing the pier apparently receding from the steamer. Why do we say 'apparently' in the latter case and not in the former? Partly because we know that the motion occurs at the fiat of the captain, who orders the engine to start but has no power to shift the pier; but mainly because the pier runs out from the solid shore, backed by the streets of the town and with miles of terra firma behind it. For these reasons we think of the steamer as 'really' moving and the motion of the pier as mere illusion.

"Now, although this explanation would satisfy the unsophisticated, all educated people since the days of Copernicus, recognize that it contains an important element of convention. The solid earth is no more than the steamer 'really' at rest; an observer on the sun would see it spinning like a fretful midge and swinging ceaselessly round in its annual orbit. If he shifted his standpoint to a fixed star he might observe that the sun itself with its train of planets is heading for the constellation Hercules. And what more do we mean by calling the star 'fixed' than that its motion, carried out in the remote depths of space, required a long period to reveal itself to terrestrial observers? In fact, in this restless and turbulent world is there anything motionless in an absolute sense and not merely in relation to something else assumed as a convenient fiction to be at rest?

"A partial answer to the question was given long ago. According to Newton's mechanics, it is at least possible to decide whether a given body is really or only apparently rotating; for if the rotation is real, the parts of a body are subject to a centrifugal force which would be absent if it were merely relative. Thus if humanity had grown up under a canopy of clouds so thick as wholly to hide the heaven and to obliterate the distinction between day and night, men of science (working by artificial light) might still have noted the bulging round the equator, have invented the experiment of Foucault's pendulum, and have observed the apparent movement of a gyroscopic axis; and from these phenomena might have deducted the existence and rate of the earth's rotation."

MOLECULAR BALANCE

Since all substance yields, inner forces must continually adjust to hold the molecules in balance. Inner forces must change to meet superimposed forces which act to increase stresses within a structure.

Not only separate parts of a structure must seek balance, but the molecules of a structure must maintain a uniform balance of inner forces to meet the external forces acting upon them. This incessant struggle is one to which we have given little thought in daily surroundings. Unless our house suffers from termites, in which molecular balance is soon lost, we rarely stop to think of the meaning this struggle carries.

THE SAFETY POINT IN MOLECULAR BALANCE

Molecular balance, as well as structural balance, is important to our welfare. The split rail over which we hope we will never have to travel, the broken automobile-axle which has caused many a serious accident, the smashed plate-glass which could not resist a good stiff gale exemplify molecular failure, imbalance of pressure stresses.

Understanding the minute preparations of all materials serving in a construction project may mean little to us, yet it is essential for our safety. For example, the rails under the stream-liner must meet the impact of outside forces. They must stand temperature changes, such as frost and thaw, as well as the ever-changing weight that is passing over them.

ANNEALING

The need to "anneal" metals and glass, that their molecular cohesion may be uniform, is one of the important preparations of these materials which enables them to serve any structure successfully. Flaws or bubbles, unseen perhaps, but injurious to the integrity of the material, may remain after pouring.

Annealing is a process of treating metal, glass, or other substances which, when cooled, must have molecular strength. Any tiny flaws in molecular consistency disappear in these substances with special treatment during slow cooling after heating. For example, steel ingots are rolled until cool to insure the rearrangement of their molecules. The large reflector for the Palomar Telescope, which was made of glass, required approximately one year to cool at the Corning Glass Works. Some metals may safely be cooled more rapidly than others, depending upon the type of previous preparation.

This annealing process equalizes the inner stresses of the material and enables it to meet a greater amount of external stress without giving way. Science must understand and meet these material requirements to insure balance and safety in all structures. Even the wooden ties used in the construction of railroad beds must have special treatment to give them molecular balance and greater resiliency and strength. Elasticity as well as strength are prerequisites for best balance in all molecular as well as cellular substances.

Compare an hour's walk on a paved highway with the same

time spent walking on a smooth dirt road and note the difference in your own fatigue. There is more "spring" in the dirt than in the asphalt. One of the reasons given for the prevalent foot troubles of modern man is the continued standing and "pounding" on hard, smooth surfaces. Molecular balance and mechanical balance are two devices of nature which must be *understood* for them to become useful in our daily living.

STRESS AND STRAIN

So long as weight is borne and movements made, stress can never be eliminated, but strains from it can be greatly reduced. In the living being one or more stresses are always present, and often all five stresses will be found. Stress is the essence of the struggle for equilibrium. Stress *acts upon* a structure, and strain is the *effect* it has upon the structure.

In the mental realm, strain results from confusion of issues. In the emotional realm, strain comes with dissatisfaction. Suppressed agitation from unnamed fears is at the root of most of our dissatisfactions.

In the mental and emotional realms the results of strain are identical. It produces imbalance in the neuromuscular mechanism and interference with smooth operation of the reciprocal muscle-groups. Restoration of balance must begin in the physical, supported by purposive mental and emotional activity.

The human body is an instrument of expression for all possible ranges of emotion and ideation. For this instrument to be effective the thinking and emotions must harmonize. There is danger in superimposing movement or position upon the body without adequate preparation in the *emotional desire*. Preparedness results from a composite of sensations organized within the body. These pass through the mental and emotional mechanisms.

Emotional appreciation must accompany the concept to effect free rhythms of response. There must be in the consciousness a sense that all is ready. All parts have fallen into line—a unit coordinated! Faith and optimism already are present.

Constructive response follows. A confidence in these inherent
mechanisms should be incorporated into our philosophy of life
to form a positive personality.

Tumbling is the first act of movement, recovery the second
act. In organized movement, opposition of all parts moving is
the third act. Opposing forces acting on the bony levers in
movement are part of this operation. The two opposing forces,
opposition of bones as weight and opposition of muscles as
power, continue to alternate in all organized movement. Adjustments may be made in the mental, emotional, chemical, or
mechanical realms, but the inevitable result will be a change
in muscular behavior. That is, we may change our thinking, our
diet, our mechanics, all in the cause of relaxation and improved
rhythms of movement. Greater satisfaction will result.

In machinery, lack of balance of parts may cause interference in operation. The wear and tear become localized and
we buy new parts. Unfortunately the human being has more
difficulty in replacing his parts. Modern science has ability to
add a few, such as eyes for the blind, red blood cells for the
anemic, but they are not only scarce but expensive and painful
to apply. We have successfully grafted bone. But who has ever
heard of grafting into the nervous system parts to generate new
energy to replace that which has been prodigally expended in
muscular tensions?

In the animal, the *crouch* muscles serve to increase pressure
upon the earth by pulling all bones backward and downward
along the axis. This increases, by tensile strength, the *compression* force acting through the thigh joints and the feet upon the
ground. With a lowered center of gravity he runs faster, fights
better. The power of the animal to spring or leap is determined
by the tensile strength in these lower body muscles. They have
the effect of increasing the poundage of pressure on the earth
through the feet. The *distance* through space covered by the

animal as he leaps is determined by the amount of pressure upon the earth by his hind legs; released suddenly, it acts upon the axis of the structure for forward, directive movement. The principle of opposition operates here.

The increased compression power in the bones due to the *tensile* power operating to draw their contacts together increases poundage in opposition to upward thrust from the ground through the feet. The compression is increased by the work of the muscles. This could be measured in foot-pounds. The sudden release of these muscles catapults the body forward. The same type of increased pressure upon the ground enables the fighting animal to maintain his stance. His supply of oxygen is also increased as the lower accessory muscles add their power to the downward pull of the diaphragm. Animal forces and mechanical forces are designed to work together in all body operations. The necessity for increasing the basic forces for survival is evident in the developed mechanisms. Both the breathing and the center of gravity must be low for survival.

In all organized motion there is an applied force operating on the separate units of weight. In one machine the force may be electricity, in another steam, in another expanding gas. In the living being it is nervous energy generated within. There are many leaks of this energy in the human body through poor balance, as there may also be in a mechanical machine if "contacts" are not "true." The parts of your automobile or your airplane must be connected and balanced one with the other so that the machinery works smoothly with least strain on its parts and with least waste of its energy fuel. Even so there are speeds that are economical and speeds that are wasteful in both the machine and the human body. If sometimes there seems to be an emphasis on the obvious, let us remember that the ideas which need the most clarification are often those to which we say "of course."

PURPOSEFUL ACTIVITY

There is but one answer to all this persistent activity. Action in life is purposeful and has creative, directive forces back of it. The future holds for man the ever-increasing experience of consciousness, and the years add to his capacity for acceptance, qualification, and control. Through knowledge, sensitive appreciation, and self-expression man continues to evolve. He forms a pattern of unity of forces, but it would be well if he were to increase his sensitiveness to the minute stimuli within, which influence his behavior, and to environmental stimuli. These together combine to affect his emotional thinking and responses. Man still lives dangerously and the habit of meeting emergencies is a part of his inheritance. The old mechanisms operate in the unconscious in their habitual way. Conscious control of conditions is only possible through recognition of the many forces involved. Through observation, and through the use of definite procedures which can be duplicated under given circumstances, we have discovered laws regarding the conditions which we should provide for ourselves in order to conserve our energies and direct them into purposeful living.

COMPARABLE PSYCHIC AND STRUCTURAL STATES

Mechanical and psychological states are not strictly comparable, but there are suggestive parallels in nervous and structural imbalances. The neurotic introvert in a state of over-attentiveness—for example, any man living his life "against the grain"—is in a state of tension. The neurotic extrovert, the one who requires travel and the swift passage of countries and people to submerge his inner self under heavy piers of new general impressions, is letting conscious life act as compression. Bending is typified in political compromise—Woodrow Wilson, Lloyd George, Winston Churchill—in crisis. Torsion is a twist in the elements of a structure. This reminds one of the gangster who twists or distorts society. Shear is a slipping, a separation, similar to the alienation produced by insanity; the nervous structure is completely dissociated.

Emotion constantly finds expression in bodily attitudes. Even when the anxiety is quite apart from the work in hand our emotional undercurrent will express itself in some bodily attitude—in the furrowed brow, the set mouth, the limited breathing, the tightly held neck muscles, or in the slumped body of discouragement or listlessness.

What makes a situation annoying? Inelasticity toward it. When reflexes are ready to act and the opportunity is present, to act is agreeable. When one is not ready to act, and is forced to act, to act is very disagreeable. The unpleasantness varies with the degree of the "set" against acting. Also, when nerves and muscles are ready to act and not allowed to act, tensions follow the inhibitions. Imbalances are established between individual parts, and opposition of movement in the muscle antagonizers become wasteful of human energy, while bones are pulled off center by these unnecessary contractions and pulls. Muscles act either concentrically or eccentrically. When acting concentrically, that is, toward center, they help to keep the bones balanced at their joints. They act as stabilizers of bony weight. When they act eccentrically they move bones away from center. Concentric action, back to the axis, tends to lower the center of gravity; eccentric to lift it. Eccentric movement shortens the axis.

CHAPTER IX

Meet Your Living Skeleton

Most of us are confidently ignorant of what is going on under our skins. Moreover, many of us exhibit a sort of squeamishness when bones and muscles are mentioned. We are happy to go about in work and play absolutely dependent upon them, but with no more curiosity about them than a domestic animal has about his anatomy. He gets along very well in his simple ignorance. Why should we bore ourselves with trying to learn anything about bones and muscles? "Leave that to the doctors," many argue. Unlike the domestic animal, however, human beings habitually manage their bones and muscles badly. Reconstructing our thinking about bones, making them live, we become conscious of their service and learn how to make the most of it to the benefit of our muscles.

THE FAMILIARITY OF GRAVITY

The human body, in addition to other requirements for living, meets the same structural problems of interacting forces as the inanimate mechanisms. Gravity acts upon the human structure as upon all other structures; weight as a force is interacting with all other forces. Measuring weight—one pound, two pounds—is man's way of measuring the action of gravity. There is the pull toward the earth and the earth's resistance to the pull. These opposing forces are equal, and their interaction keeps us upon the surface of the earth.

Man is pulled toward the center of the earth, but the earth resists his weight with equal force or he would sink into its center. The friendly and beneficent power of gravity, which helps to keep the universe in order, aids the human body in all its movements. You do not take account of gravity through any action of logic. You learn about it in childhood by many a hard bump. Making quick adjustments becomes a habit, so that your body responds unconsciously to the most gentle hint of gravity. You are thus protected by your inner mechanisms. These mechanisms take care of the balance of the body as a whole, but often through false conceptions we waste much energy holding individual parts out of balance, making it harder for the whole to function.

HOW WEIGHT IS SUPPORTED

There are but three ways known to man for the support of weights; weights sit, hang, or are braced. In the human body the head sits, the ribs hang, the pelvis is braced. Supported at different levels, all our body weights are either sitting on something below, hanging from something above, or being braced by something at the sides. Knowing how these weights are transferred one to the other is important for a clear picture of ourselves in balance. Bone balance saves muscular energy.

When a weight sits it must be so adjusted to its supporting surface that its center of gravity falls over the middle third of its supporting base. Thus it sits with stability. If a weight is hanging, the central axis of the suspended weight—the shortest distance between two points along the vertical—must fall directly under its support. The separate hanging units of the body must have this condition established to ensure free motion when energy is applied. If a weight is supported at the sides, namely buttressed, there is formed an arch. The braces or buttresses press against the keystone of the arch, thus acting upon it from the sides.

The two thigh bones act as buttresses bracing against their sockets at each side of the *front of the pelvis,* and through them to the keystone at the *back,* the *sacrum.* The upward thrust at the sides must balance the downward thrust at the supporting surface of the keystone, the sacrum, where the upper spine sits upon it.

MECHANICAL FUNCTION OF BONES

The mechanical function of bones is to support weight and to serve as levers for movement. A lever is a rod free to turn about a fulcrum. All bones which can move about their joints are to be considered as levers.

Our consciousness of mastery of arms and legs has more of bone consciousness in it than we usually recognize. In every movement there is weight displacement; that is, bone displacement. Given the location of a bone, a predetermined direction for movement and the *desire to move,* any bony lever will respond by means of nerves and muscles. The response is automatic. *We move bones.*

PRINCIPLES OF BALANCE

There are three conditions which must be met in all structures to assure their balance. In stacking baby's blocks, in designing the stories of a building, or in arranging the units of the human body, there should be a broad level base, and each weight should be near the central axis and as near the base of support as will conform with the structure. In proportion as these three conditions are established in any structure, stability is increased and the center of gravity is lowered. Greater security and flexibility are gained.

In the upright stance of the human body some of the requirements for stability cannot be met so perfectly as in a static structure. If they were, man of necessity would have much greater bulk, cumbersome joints, and slower movement.

WEIGHT UNITS OF THE BODY

In the human framework there are three units or masses of weight, roughly comparable to the stories of a building. They are the skull or head, the thorax or rib-case, and the pelvis, which forms the actual base. Even though these three weights should be in good alignment with each other, they do not sit one upon the other. *The spinal column connects the three.* It supports the weight of the head above it, of the rib-case at its sides, and transfers the weight of the two into the pelvis at the center back, the sacrum. All body weights either sit or hang on the spine and are carried to the pelvis *by way of the spine.* No weight travels downward through the front of the body. There is no bone in the abdominal wall.

The arms and legs may be considered as appendages to the main units of weight and as such are used in expansive movements of the body. Thus the weight of the spine entering the pelvis at the back is managed and controlled by the back thrust of the legs at their sockets at the front of the pelvis, and moved by means of their muscular attachments to the spine and pelvis.

THE SPINAL COLUMN

A strut is an upright support; a girder is a horizontal support. In the four-legged position the spinal column served man as a girder. All weights hung from it. In the upright position the spine must serve in a vertical plane. It is competent, however, in either plane because of the design of its *curves.* Weights still hang upon it and are controlled in the upright position through the axis of its opposing curves.

According to mechanical law, a flexible rod, to support weight in an upright position, must assume opposing curves and must cross the vertical axis of its load in at least two places, the number of places depending upon the number of curves. This forms an axis of support. The spine has four curves; directed forward in the region of the neck, the *cervical* curve; directed backward in the region of the rib-case, the *thoracic* curve; forward in the region of the waist, the *lumbar* curve; and backward in the lowest part, the sacrum, which forms the keystone at the back of the pelvic arch. The spine is under the center of the weight of the skull. The head *sits* upon it. Lower down under the weight of both the skull and rib-case, it again comes to center. Both centers fall in the axis produced by the spinal curves. Mechanically, it is completely qualified to carry all the weights of the upper body and more. This is done by all forces within its curves opposing each other across its long vertical axis.

An astonishing number of persons hold strange notions about their spines. Misled by the row of bony buttons just under the skin on the back, they think of the spine as a thin, flattish, surface arrangement. Giving it no depth in their imagination, they have no sense of its value as a *supporting column* in their consciousness. It is, in fact, composed of a series of thick, strong vertebrae, increasing in size from the top downward to its base. These are connected by thick cushions of cartilage (intervertebral discs), which add flexibility and shock-absorbing power to the column. Vertebrae, through their discs, sit one upon the other. They are held together by ligaments and muscles and extend well toward the center of the body *in all parts*, but especially so in the two places mentioned above. The opposing forces of the spinal curves would be unable to maintain the upright of the flexible column if the weight it supports did not fall at the central axis in two or more places.

With its adjoined muscles and ligaments the spine forms a round, flexible column with its four opposing curves, and is much longer and larger around than is commonly supposed. Where it assumes its lower forward curve and weights upon it are heaviest, it measures three to five inches in diameter. In fact, the front aspect of the spine at this level is equidistant from the "buttons" of the spine at the back to the inner surface of the front abdominal wall. The spine comes to the center of the body at this region, and can be felt easily through the relaxed abdominal wall of a thin person.

THE LINE OF GRAVITY —
TRIANGLES OF OPPOSING CURVES

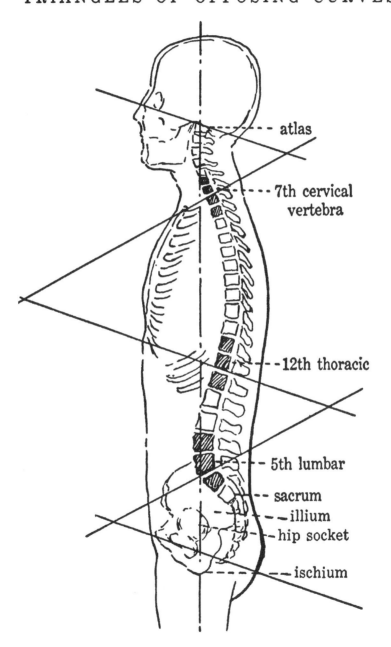

atlas

7th cervical
vertebra

12th thoracic

5th lumbar

sacrum

illium

hip socket

ischium

One of the disfiguring marks of poor bony alignment which annoys the designer of your clothing is the lack of balance of the cervical region, the neck of the spine. The lowest of the cervical vertebrae can easily be felt just about where the back collar-button comes, if you are a man, or just below where the catch lies on the strand of pearls gracing a lady's neck. This is called the *vertebra prominens*. In many older people and in careless younger ones it presents an ugly reminder of poor balance of the upper back and neck.

The spine not only supports weights but it is the focal point of all movement; a powerful muscular "python" carrying the body weight about; bending and twisting in response to its needs! Every movement of arms and legs must coordinate in balanced rhythm through the spine. Keep the weights centered in the spine, that greater departure from center may be possible when movement takes place. In alternate action of all parts in opposition, natural rhythms carry through. The spine controls all movement and absorbs all body shocks. Thus it helps the rest of the bony framework to stabilize the body in all radial muscle activity in expanded movement of arms and legs. Back your ribs into your spine without bending it or lowering the chest. Stay with your spine.

THE PELVIS

The terms sacrum, ilium, pubic arch, and ischium, and their whereabouts *in the pelvis* should become as familiar to us as jaw bone, collar bone, and breast bone. We need to know them in order to be intelligent about economy of bodily movement and support. They form the base of our structure and carry and move the greatest amount of weight. We should know how to manage them.

What people commonly call their "hip bones," the *ilia*, form the sides of the pelvis. Their upper ridge is frequently used as a resting-place for the hands. By extending the thumb backward and the fingers forward, the hand fits easily over the top curving rim of the ilium. These sides of the pelvis form a pelvic rim by joining with the sacrum at the back and with narrow bones at the front connected to the pubis. *Pelvis* is the old Latin word for basin. While it is a basin in the sense of containing the lower viscera and many muscles of movement, including breathing-muscles, it is mainly as a supporting structure that it serves the body in stance and movement. It catches all the top weights that the legs must carry about.

The ilia fit snugly against each side of the wedge-shaped sacrum, the lowest part of the spinal column. The contacting surfaces of both ilia and sacrum are very irregular in shape. Their surfaces remind one of the irregularity of the surfaces of the two sides of a waffle iron, although with less orderly arrangement. Bumps of one fit into the hollows of the other. Their meeting-place is known as the sacroiliac joint. Strong ligaments bind these bones firmly together and there is a minimum chance of one slipping on the other, though some gliding movement is possible. Very often, the complaint of "slipped sacroiliac," with accompanying pain, is merely a strain in soft tissues around these joints, due to imbalance in transferring weight from pelvis to legs. In many cases rest and better balance is all that is needed.

The *pubis* is the front part of the pelvic rim. As stated, its extensions, called *rami,* connect the hip bones with the pubic arch in front, completing the pelvic rim. The inferior rami connect the pubic arch with the bones we sit upon, the *ischia.*

When sitting, one can reach under the body on each side and feel the ischia. These the Germans call the "sit-bones," and they are *to be sat upon,* although few of us follow this advice, preferring to slump on our spines or brace ourselves in our knees. Both of these positions are very fatiguing to the spinal column, especially at its base. When sitting, sink deep into your chair and let your bones support you.

The ischium forms the lowest part of the hip bone on each side. It meets the other two bones of the hip, the ilium and pubis, to form the deep socket into which is cupped the head of the thigh bone. At birth the three parts of the hip bone are separate, but they fuse during childhood so that the socket has a continuous bony surface in its hollow cup.

The ischia are located farther to the front and lower in the pelvic basin than many realize. They are appreciably lower

Where Body Weight Sits

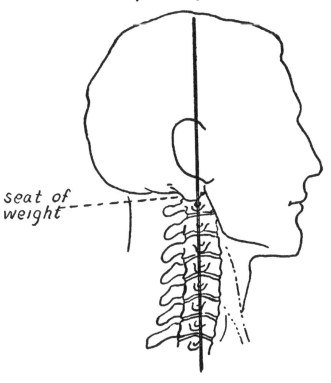

seat of
weight

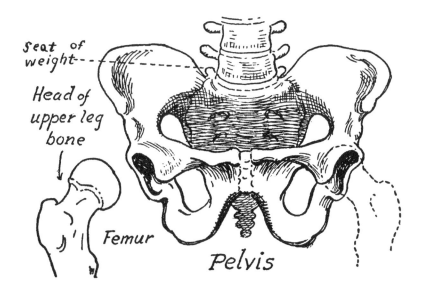

seat of
weight

Head of
upper leg
bone

Femur

Pelvis

than the end of the spine; in fact, these are the lowest bones in the body when sitting. By sitting deep into the sit-bones (ischia), we balance the pelvis to support its spinal load. The ischia should be in a plane with the center of the thigh joints to insure two equal lines of force directed toward the center of the thigh joints and so to the keystone, the sacrum.

In good balance, whether *sitting or standing,* the direction of leg thrust through the thigh joint to the sacral keystone must be the same. Only by balancing the forces in the pelvis can we reduce strain in soft tissues. The body cannot have one special line of support through which the sacral keystone is held in place under its load when sitting and another when standing. It must conform to certain structural relationship *in all positions* to carry its spinal load. *Its center of gravity relates similarly to the sacrum in both sitting and standing.*

When sitting deep in the ischia, weight neither thrusts forward into the knees nor slides backward upon the lower spine. Often we either rock too far forward on the ischia in an effort to "sit tall," thus throwing our weight into the thighs and forward into the knees somewhat as weight rests on the rockers of a forward-tipping rocking-chair, or we rock backward on the ischia—the reverse picture of the rocking-chair—until we rest on the end of the spine. In the well-balanced pelvis, when sitting weight should be delivered to the chair from the sacrum by way of the sit-bones, with least weight on the thighs. Otherwise, our legs continue to support part of our weight—a wasteful use of energy. All four legs of the chair should receive equal shares of our weight.

To locate the thigh joints *when sitting,* spread the thumb and fingers apart and place them low in the front of the body where the acute angle is formed by the trunk and thighs. The tips of the thumb and middle finger will be over the thigh joints.

Frequently a bony bump low on the side of the hip bone is mistaken for the thigh joint. The thigh joints are not on the sides. They are at the side front of the pelvis. This bump, the *great trochanter,* is a part of the thigh bone. To locate the great trochanter put a thumb on the center of the crest of the hip bone at the side of the body, extend the middle finger straight downward, in line with the location of the side seam of trousers, and it will rest on the great trochanter. The neck of this bone extends inward and toward the front, to insert into the hip *socket* to form the thigh joint. The thigh joints lie much closer to the central line of the front of the body than do the bony bumps often mistaken for them. *The thigh joints are but a hand span apart across the front of the pelvis.*

The sacrum at birth is composed of separate vertebrae which soon fuse together to make one complete wedge-shaped bone with its point directed downward. It acts as a keystone for the pelvic arch. It is held in place at the back of the pelvis, like the keystone of any arch, by pressure from the sides through the sacroiliac joints.

The pelvis is a firm base for support of body weights. Limited movement of its parts is allowed by the two sacroiliac joints and at the joining of the two pubic bones in front. Some movement in all directions is allowed between the pelvis and the lowest movable vertebra of the spine, the *fifth lumbar,* but the most marked amount of movement of any joints of the pelvis occurs at the thigh joints. These, being rotary joints, can catch and move weight in any direction.

THE INTEGRATED TRUNK

What we call the *trunk*—in art circles, the torso—is the main part of the body without head and limbs; it consists of the rib-case and pelvis, connected by the spinal column.

When all weights, excluding the extremities, are drawn together toward their supporting structure, the spine, we have all parts integrated into a compact mass. This is cylindrical in shape and its contents are enclosed in a well-integrated body wall. The body wall is flexible, however, and this causes many of man's structural troubles.

Since there are no bones in the front wall of the abdominal cavity, it is as impossible for the accumulated body-weights to be directly transferred to the base of the pelvis through this area as it would be to pass those of a building through a wall of stretched canvas. These weights must inevitably, therefore, hang from the spine and travel downward by way of the spine and pelvis to the lower extremities. All top weights, except the head, *hang* on the flexible, competent, spinal column. The integration of the trunk depends upon our letting them do so. Draw the ribs back to the spine; draw the abdomen back to the spine—thus make it easier for the spine to *manage the weights it must support.*

WHERE THE HEAD SITS

Whether standing, sitting, or lying down, we have a problem to face in getting the head in the most comfortable position. For best balance we must locate the place where the head really rests, the bone on which it sits. Put the tip of a finger of each hand in the hollow under each ear-lobe, between the hinge of the jawbone and the skull. A rod joining fingertips would run through the place where the head sits on, and forms a joint with, the top vertebra of the spine. Let it sit here and rock upon its cradle.

Many have the impression that the *back* of the head rests on the spine. This is false. In our upright position it could never be balanced if this were true. When an object sits, its support must be under the *center of its weight*. The top bone of the spine must, for good balance, be centered under the weight of the head. This top vertebra is called the *atlas*. Like the patient old giant after which it is named, it carries a world—not *the* world, but what is more important to each, his own world—and its balance is essential.

The atlas is a small bone about an inch and a half across, with two tiny "cradles" on its upper surface at either side. Into these fit two smooth, rounded, bony protuberances from the center of the base of the skull. These are called the *occipital condyles*. They rest on, and can rock backward and forward in, the "cradles" of the atlas.

THE RIB-CASE

Another thing which must be pictured clearly before the balance of our bony framework can be fully understood is the formation of the rib-case or thorax. Few of us realize that the ribs *hang* from the spine. At least, they do if they are allowed to. The law of gravity will operate effectively in this matter provided the owner of the ribs can bring himself to trust it.

The rib-case is designed to protect the internal mechanisms, the lungs, the heart, and the blood vessels, housed within its cavity. It consists of twenty-four curved, bladelike bones, twelve on each side. They are attached in pairs to the twelve vertebrae of the thoracic spine and, except for the two lower "floating ribs," to the breast bone at the front.

The twelve pairs of ribs are not made wholly of bone throughout their length, but in front have cartilaginous attachments, from one to six inches in length, to the breast bone. Their line of direction is first backward from their joints at the spine, then sideways and downward, then swings forward to the front where they join their sternal cartilages, the cartilages attached to the "sternum" or breast bone. Some ribs are as much as six inches lower in the front than at the level of their vertebral joinings. As in the four-legged position, they still hang. They are movable at both ends. This, in addition to their curved design and to their cartilaginous portions, affords great flexibility to the thorax (chest).

The curve of each circling rib is most marked at the back of the rib-case, at the part known as the angle of the ribs." Because of these angles of the ribs, the inside of the thorax presents a cavity on each side of the spine, extending well back of the front face of the spine. A major share of the lungs lies in this region, in the depths of the ribs in the back. In fact, a greater number of lung cells lie behind the midplane of the body than in front of it, where the heart and its vessels occupy a goodly portion of the chest space.

It is important for us to understand the shape of the rib-case. It is conical, not spherical. Its shape is like that of a lemon, not that of an orange. One of the most important results of allowing the ribs to hang, thus establishing mobility at their two ends—at the spinal joints and at their cartilage attachments in front—is to maintain this conical shape, which is best suited for the housing of the organic contents.

Further benefits of the freely hanging ribs are many. When the chest is conical the greatest possible vertical and front-to-back depth of the thoracic cavity is attained. These depths are important, both for the free downward excursion of the diaphragm and for the freedom of circulation in the large blood-vessels within the chest cavity. The diaphragm serves as a floor for the thorax and a roof for the stomach and liver. It moves *up and down* in breathing. By itself it cannot move sidewise.

When the ribs are balanced at the spine they hang freely, and have their fullest range of motion. This means flexibility in all the *one hundred and four* to *one hundred and eight* joints of the rib-case. Mobility at these many joinings allows free use of the lung cells on both sides of the spine in respiration, and gives room for free circulation in the blood vessels to heart and lungs. This also aids the spine in the support of its weight loads. Two more highly important benefits occur with the conical-shaped rib-case. The top of the breast bone will be well forward, to give the shoulder girdle proper support at the joints where the collar bones, the *clavicles*, are joined to it. Also the position of the first three ribs will be relatively horizontal, giving front-to-back depth in the upper chest-cavity. Balanced adjustment between shoulder girdle and top ribs is necessary for the natural alignment of the blood vessels supplying the arms and head. These blood vessels pass over the top of the first rib to supply the arms and upward to supply the head; unbalanced relationship between ribs and collar bones, therefore, interferes with blood supply to the arms and to the head.

WHAT TO DO WITH OUR CHESTS

There are many popular notions about what we should *do* about the "chest" and shoulders. In early training most of us have been warned frequently to lift and expand the chest; to hold the shoulders back. In our efforts to follow such directions we have not only added muscular strain to poor bone-balance, but we have distorted the natural shape and flexibility of the rib-case, and disturbed our breathing-apparatus.

When we respond to any of the typical commands, such as "chest up," "shoulders back," "head up," "stand tall," we most often make the changes by bringing the *lower end* of the breast bone forward and up. *This depresses its top end* and interferes with the support and balance of the shoulder girdle at its sternal attachments, the *sterno-clavicular* joints, where the collar bones and breast bones meet.

We raise the ribs by the pull of lateral muscles that are attached to higher bones, making the ribs higher and wider than necessary when in their natural, balanced position at their own levels at the spine. This adds their weight to a higher point on the spine and this same weight must again pass down through the very spinal levels from which it has been pulled. Our center of gravity has thus been lifted, and we literally "hang by the neck." The end result is a hard, fixed, expanded, high chest, which involves great strain and tension in the rib-case and in the spinal column. The spinal axis, instead of being lengthened, is shortened by crowding together the upper thoracic vertebrae. Slumping is bound to result from this fatiguing, holding process in which muscles have taken on the work which bones should be doing.

Of all this strain we are quite unconscious. We have become habituated to the two alternates—slumping or chest elevation. We have a sense of guilt for the first, and quickly apply the second as a remedy. Thus we daily spend much energy unnecessarily, shifting from one of these unbalanced positions to the other. Bone balance and spinal control is the only answer to such problems of bodily strain. Relaxation is to be found in balance. *Stay with your spine.*

APPENDAGES TO THE TRUNK

Legs and arms are necessary to the spine in the arrangement of our framework, but their strength and cooperation depend upon the closeness of association with the spine. Through deep-lying muscles, fascial sheets, and ligaments which connect all parts to each other, this association is accomplished.

Power and movement of the arms in throwing, grasping, or lifting outside weights are dependent upon spinal support and the underlying support and strength of the pelvic base. In the bones of the pelvis resides the "ballast" for structural support in movement, and in the *crouch muscles* of loins and thighs lies the ability to hold the stance and absorb the shocks of all expanded movement of both arms and legs. In holding the stance this bony and muscular base moves the least, but works the hardest. The shoulders and arms, as well as the rib-case, are all connected with the strong lower levels of the spine.

The shoulder girdle is not a supporting part of the body unit. It is superimposed upon the rest of the bony framework. Its bones are attached to the framework at the *manubrium,* a small bone at the top of the breast bone, to which the shoulder girdle is attached. Except for the joinings at this attachment the shoulder girdle has no fixed attachment to any bone of the skeleton. The shoulder blades and collar bones move freely over the surface of the chest wall. The shoulder girdle hangs mainly by muscles from the head and upper spine. If the shoulder girdle structure is balanced, this arrangement gives the arms a chance to swing freely without pulling unevenly upon the rib structure or the neck muscles.

The shoulder structure is amply supported and will repose quite comfortably in its muscular sling if we allow the shoulders to hang and refrain from holding them in forced, unnatural positions. The shoulder joints are rotary joints. When contacting bones of rotary joints are in balance the surrounding muscles operate very much as the spokes of a revolving wheel. There is movement and support through *any radius from hub to circumference.* In free thigh and shoulder joints we have all these possibilities during expanded movement. These thigh and shoulder joints are the only rotary joints in the body. How these connect and work with spinal control is shown in a later chapter.

CHAPTER X

Mechanisms for Ease and Efficiency

Mechanisms developed in response to the survival urge are inherited by man. These mechanisms help us to withstand the strains of the strenuous living of our times.

The evidence of prolonged strain may be observed every day in the face and body of modern man. Such evidence lies in involuntary contraction of neck, shoulder, and chest muscles, in aborted breathing, in useless movement, in stooped bodies with accompanying sagging spirits, and in irritable and impatient reactions. These various manifestations of tension come from central reflexes, developed as survival mechanisms, but operating in modern man in response to anxieties and pressures of living. They exist in the memory patterns of prehistoric *preparations* for danger. Today they organize into "floating anxieties."

The human animal works in all his "pull-up" muscles whenever his attention is challenged, and challenge is almost constant, either by his environment or by his own mental activity. Since he is "civilized," his expansive responses are inhibited; he has accustomed himself to holding on to himself. The sequence is lost in the cycle of responses for danger. The first phase of survival response is alertness, the second, decision and preparation, and the third, response. It becomes more and more difficult in modern man to find some satisfactory form of expression in the third phase of survival response, that of movement. "Alertness" is continued, the preparation stage is never experienced. Such "holding" is prolonged from day to day; it is seldom completely lost, even in sleep, as it has become *an entirely unconscious but anxious way of life.* Thus tensions accumulate, with all their disturbing effects on the various bodily systems. They should be dissolved in action.

STAGES OF RESPONSE TO THE SURVIVAL URGE

Alertness is the first response to awareness of possible danger. In the animal the head is raised for the keenest use of his senses, particularly of eyes, nose, and ears. If necessary, he rises on his hind legs to increase the environmental range of his stimuli. If he finds that no danger exists he returns to his peaceful activity.

But if danger presents itself, the second response to the survival urge occurs—that of preparation for flight or fight. In either response, conservation of energy, efficient use of power, and rapid feeding of active body cells will be needed. Tensions of the alerted stage break up immediately as preparation for activity takes place in the unconscious mechanisms. Deep muscles become active in lowering weight along the spine toward the pelvis and hind legs. Thus the center of gravity is lowered and control in the crouch muscles is promoted. Breathing becomes deeper and faster, for oxygen will be needed to feed active cells throughout the body. The diaphragm in its deep excursions must do its part in assisting the flow of venous blood and lymph back to the lungs. The wastes of burning must be hurried out in order that fresh fuel and oxygen may be supplied to the cells. Adrenalin and other hormones needed to speed activity and increase the power of muscles are poured into the blood stream. These unconscious mechanisms quickly prepare the animal to protect himself from danger.

The third stage, that of extreme activity in fighting or running, employs effectively all the muscular powers of the animal to carry him through to safety. Those with the best survival mechanisms survive.

One of the most important factors in the preparation phase for survival is the mechanical one, that of lowering the center of gravity. Many devices have been developed for this low-set function of the animal framework, among them the diaphragm connections with deep abdominal and pelvic muscles and their fascial sheets. They make it possible for the crouch muscles and the pelvic-floor muscles to work with the diaphragm, not only to enable the animal to hold his stance, but to aid the vascular system in its need for freer functioning, and to release the upper muscles of thorax (chest), neck, and arms for directive, expansive movement. All *upper* accessory muscles for breathing have to be freed for these active services. Quick action of all moving parts is necessary.

Still another preparation function to aid in lowering the stance is that of growling or hissing. We think of these sounds as merely warnings to the enemy. But close observation will reveal that they are made by deep, inside muscles which act to lower the center of gravity. Even in our domestic animals we can observe the menacing look, almost like cringing, accompanying the growl or the hiss. That look may be seen to be a withdrawing action along the spine toward the pelvis, and if it is continued to an extreme it results in the crouch position, as we have all seen in two cats ready to spring in an alley fight. Hissing between the teeth is a valuable exercise today for relaxation.

MODERN MAN IN THE "ALERTED" STAGE

Modern man often suspends himself in the state of alertness for danger. This continues when there is indecision or uncertainty. It is a state of *inhibition of response*, with high center of gravity, breathing abated, action inhibited. Bodily systems are cooperating, as is their habit in a suspended state of fear-anxiety. Activity is needed. Any activity that will use the mechanisms of response is better than none. But activity should not take the line of anxiety. The pattern of suspense must be broken. It is much wiser to engage in some form of expanded activity which will break up the tensions, and then to go back refreshed to your problem. This allows completion of the three phases of survival response—alertness, preparation, activity. Rest follows.

The height of the center of gravity of man's body is a fair index of his state of tension. If it could be read as precisely as the mercury in a thermometer it would be relatively easy to determine when imbalances exist in the function and interplay of the various systems of the body. The high center of gravity occurring with states of tension can be noted, however, in uneven breathing rhythms, mostly chest breathing.

Learn to recognize your own symptoms. Increase your awareness of the danger signals. Learn to correct them before they control you. This exemplifies *your command* versus *their control.*

The continued expression of the tensions of the alerted stage may project itself into hysteria. Many of us suffer from forms of hysteria, but would be quite indignant if we were told the truth. We all suffer from it at times when we are careless and allow these tensions to accumulate. The very fact that some are afraid to cultivate their own "awareness" is an unconscious evidence of the presence of hysteria. Learn the facts about your bodily systems and live with the facts—your imagination will do the rest.

HYSTERIA AND INHIBITED REFLEXES

The continued "pulling up" of alertness is hysteria, a state in which one can no longer lower the diaphragm on the spine for a good deep breath. *Hysteria is emotional preparation for movement, with continued inhibition of movement.* When the alerted stage is maintained, the downward action of the diaphragm is limited. We have all experienced the short, jerky breathing of hysteria. This interferes with active inherited reflexes, confusions arise, and toxins are stored in the tissues. Man becomes self-doubting, self-conscious, afraid. He extends his fear through the present into the future. His fear lives with him all the time, but varies its expression by changing its content— one day he is afraid of office problems, another day afraid of home situations, another day afraid of sleeplessness. There is a vast array.

If in childhood or youth a person fails to get what he wants or to do what he wants to do, and this thwarting continues, it often turns inward. Confusions and inability to find satisfactory expression arise. Such a situation may develop an egocentric person. We often say that he has a "chip on his shoulder," or he is hypersensitive, envious, or jealous. Any or all of these fruits of the disappointed ego may be present. He has long since forgotten his early disappointment, but it lies deep within, and only his negative manifestations rise in his consciousness to pester him. He is desperately trying in every way to support his ego, and the fear that he is not succeeding haunts him.

There are often very subtle ways in which he manipulates his environment and those in it to get the satisfactions needed for the support of his ego, to allay the deep-set fears of his own uncertainties. When these efforts are not effective real hysteria often raises its head, and a good dose of cold water is required to get the organism functioning again in coordinated movement. Such a person is himself very miserable, and his family equally so. He is often disgusted with himself and yet does not probe deeply enough into the unconscious background to arrive at some of the causes or at the means of prevention. He is afraid of himself, although he does not recognize it, and would not confess to it if he did. He turns his sharp tongue upon others to prove his courage. Often organic rhythms are disturbed in hysteria. These may be considered serious organic maladies by friends and family but, in fact, *are rarely so.*

Through intellectual pride man has dulled his protective mechanisms. His sensory organism must be revived and his responsive mechanisms freed. His knowledge of the meaning of "self-control" and of body balance can then be of real benefit to him. He can move off surplus energy from overacting muscles and redistribute energy to vital muscles inhibited by bodily or emotional imbalances.

In all man's emotional anxieties (his phases of fear), the diaphragm tends to give way to the upper accessory muscles—those which stretch the body upward for better observation, for better use of eye and ear: the *alerted stage*. Chest and head are high and the center of gravity is raised, accompanied by high breathing. When anxiety continues, the center of gravity remains high and the upper accessory muscles of breathing, those of shoulders and chest, act to widen and lift the chest, and thus *diaphragm depth is lessened*.

The interference with the deep excursion of the diaphragm disconnects its action with its lower structural muscles in abdomen and pelvis, and thus one of its important functions is lost—that of a vascular agent. Also its pressure on stomach and liver is reduced and its service as an agent of digestion is lost.

THE DIAPHRAGM

There are many mistaken ideas regarding the diaphragm and how it works. The diaphragm is a muscular and tendonous structure, of dome shape. When relaxed it looks somewhat like an open umbrella, with handle extending down the spine. It forms the floor of the chest cavity, the roof of the abdominal cavity. Its circumferential border interdigitates, like interlocking fingers, with the deepest muscle of the abdominal wall, the *transversalis*. It is pistonlike in its action, bulging upward inside the cylindrical body-canal when it is relaxed in expiration, then downward when it contracts in inspiration. It deepens the chest space and stimulates peristalsis (the action of the digestive muscles) in its downward journey; on its release the transversalis contracts. These alternate movements change the vascular pressures in the abdominal cavity and increase circulation throughout the body.

As its name would imply, the transversalis muscle passes horizontally across the abdomen and when contracted acts as a "belly band." Its contraction aids in moving the blood from the deep abdominal vessels into the large vein, the *vena cava,* which travels, with the thoracic duct containing lymph, upward *through the diaphragm* in front of the spine to the thorax, where these vessels must give up their toxic wastes to the lungs. The transversalis contracts on exhalation.

The diaphragm has no power to move sideways. It is not made that way. It can no more push the ribs sideways than the two sides of your tongue can simultaneously push your two cheeks outward. All motions of the tongue are made in relation to its longitudinal tendon, which extends forward from its attachment to the hyoid bone (the bone you can feel at the "Adam's Apple") to the tip. Short muscular fibers of the tongue contract crosswise *toward this tendon* for moving the tip wherever we want it to go. A similar action is true of your diaphragm. It contracts always *downward through its long tendons at the spine.* Hence, when you widen and lift your ribs in breathing you are using upper superficial muscles, *not the diaphragm.*

The diaphragm must move down the spine to increase the depth of the chest cavity. In doing this it is joined by its lower accessory muscles, deep abdominal and pelvic muscles. These pelvic muscles spread out on the inner surface and floor of the pelvic structure and form a complete inner muscular wall. Some of them anchor to the thigh bones at the front and some of them extend well up the spine to the lowest thoracic vertebra, lying close to, and parallel with, the tendons of the diaphragm. Deep fascia connects them and helps to stabilize their functioning.

It is through the office of these pelvic muscles that fighting animals and men boxing or wrestling are able to hold their stance, to lower the center of gravity and at the same time, through the deep use of the diaphragm, aid the quick removal of waste from the tissues and the resupply of oxygen needed for the rapidly burning fuel in the active muscles.

The muscles of locomotion and of the diaphragm developed together. This must be so or survival would not have been possible. The animal who held his center of gravity low wasted less fuel and energy. By returning lymph and venous blood back to the lungs, he prevented his mechanism from clogging and supplied fuel and oxygen quickly to the hungry, fighting cells. If his chest and neck muscles pulled up in the fight faster or harder than the stance muscles pulled down, they interfered with the diaphragm's excursions down the spine and the stance muscles could not hold the center of gravity low, nor could the diaphragm supply the burning muscles with enough oxygen. Thus we see that all these lower muscles serve the diaphragm, and in turn the diaphragm serves them. Balanced cooperation! By changing our ideas about posture we can establish the natural functioning of these mechanisms in modern living.

THE LUNGS

The lungs have no part in the motivating function of taking a breath. Any change in the shape of the thoracic wall that would tend to increase the unoccupied space gives atmospheric pressure a chance to help fill the lungs. Atmospheric pressure is an aid in breathing. The lungs will receive air no matter what the shape of the cavity housing them.

Even though we often talk as if we breathed with our lungs, this of course is not true. The lungs are passive members in breathing. Their organic function is to lend the surfaces of their millions of cells to exchange of gases through their membranes. They can do this very effectively in the space allowed by *any shape* that the chest wall might assume. *The shape of this cavity is not important in the functioning of the lungs.* Either a round, wide chest cavity or a long, deep one offers adequate opportunity to the lungs. *Movement of air* throughout the entire lung surface is far more important than the quantity of oxygen inhaled, for the lungs always have their residue of oxygen.

So far as the lungs are concerned, we are not interested in whether the upper accessory muscles aid in breath-getting, or the lower accessory muscles of pelvis and spine aid the diaphragm in its work. What we are interested in is a low center of gravity and the best cooperation of all muscles in their effects on the circulatory mechanisms. Such cooperation insures speedy elimination of waste and adequate cell-feeding. Low, deep breathing results in a low center of gravity.

Our concerns in modern life are release from tension, the return of natural rhythms to the muscles, cell feeding, more confidence in living. If these are our goals then we must know what the different changes in the shape of the thorax mean to the nervous system, to the muscles, and to the vascular system. We have seen that a spherical chest fixes the many joints of the thorax, disturbs the balanced relationship of spine, pelvis, and thighs, raises the center of gravity, and robs the diaphragm and the transversalis of their freest action. It favors shallow breathing, which does not allow free circulation of air in the lungs, or good circulation of blood to and from the spinal cord or in the abdomen. The more action in the body wall through free, articular, bony joinings, *the more movement of both blood and air.*

IMPORTANCE OF CIRCULATION

Most of our blood vessels are muscular. Blood has to be propelled about through the structure. If skeletal muscles are tense, hard, fixed, their unchanging pressure on blood vessels and capillaries makes it difficult for the blood to permeate through the tissues, return to the veins, and move back to the heart. Circulation is impeded, cell feeding reduced, and the elimination of wastes is greatly slowed. Toxins accumulate.

Circulation in blood vessels and the heart is aided by the deep excursions of the diaphragm, and its action with the lower associated muscles and their connective fascia. The cooperative functioning of these mechanisms "milks" the venous blood and lymph from the lower tissues and returns it to the thorax. Wherever blood vessels are, there lymph vessels will also be found.

The heart pumps the blood, full of nutriment and oxygen, through the arteries to all cells of the body. But the lymph and venous blood returning to the lungs with their load of toxins resulting from the fires of burning have no heart pump behind them. Muscles must aid these vascular vessels to perform their important task. The function of the diaphragm, the transversalis, and lower muscular structures is a most important aid in this necessary flow of venous blood and of lymph.

If it can be said that any parts of the body burn more rapidly than others it is the muscles of upper thigh, lower back, and pelvis as we sit, stand, or walk in most of our daily activities. The responsibility of weight transference lies in these parts. They receive the hardest tasks and accumulate in their muscles the greatest amount of fatigue poisons.

The largest vascular structures lie close to the bones for protection, for good circulation; therefore the *sleeve of muscles* around all bones should be active, not static. Their pressure against and upon bones must be reduced. Hold your bones loosely and rebalance them often at their points of support. Activity need not necessarily be expressed in expanded motion, but all body parts should be free to move in any direction possible to them. This is equilibrium—ease and potential energy stored as one! Relaxation!

With a low center of gravity, with muscles of the base and of the diaphragm cooperating to control and pass the spinal loads safely through to the legs, neither animal nor man suffers the instability caused by "top-pulls." If this be true, then all functioning is aided by operating along these lines. Know where your bones are supported; bring weight frequently back to their centers of support, and so lower the center of gravity. Avoid distortion of the trunk; avoid bending in such a way that some part of the spinal column is used as a *hinge.* The spinal axis must remain straight and long; bending shortens it. Study procedures that promote balance of the bones, thus producing free activity in the spinal column. Travel through your skeletal framework in your imagination and watch it make adjustments. Changes will result. Balance and relaxation will become realities!

CHAPTER XI

Body Patterns and Poses

A man's posture can change for spring and for fall. People have different gaits for Sundays and for weekdays. A man does not walk to suicide as he walks to marriage, and the under-bookkeeper does not walk into the president's office in the manner in which he enters his own apartment. Posture holds the life of charm and efficiency. It gives sparkle to the eyes, lift to the face, and lilt to the voice.

A person has cycles of buoyancy, depression, or indifference which he expresses by his body attitudes as his life changes. The set thinker has set muscles; inhibition and aggressiveness pass through the same body and come out in their familiar attitudes.

A country boy, hands in pocket and gait rolling, walks differently almost as soon as he is on the paved street. Any man used to country lanes finds that the city changes his physical balances and his gait; the determination to get to an appointment sweeps him there; it becomes more and more unusual for him to stay still. He wears his new clothes all the time; he pays some attention to fashion; he kneels no more in the fields; his exercise is done to the accompaniment of the radio or television;

his body expression has changed. His center of gravity is higher. He has joined the city throng of automobilists who use the cervical spine to the neglect of the lumbar, and the straphangers who travel on their arms.

The Greeks had a feeling for balance. Dynamic symmetry was in their bones. The Romans began to stress the superficial—big muscles and large chests were important to express the glory of the conquerer. The military emphasis increased from that time forth, eventually lending its influence to ideals of posture. Bombast replaced simplicity.

In the latter part of the last century military drill, called "gymnastic drill," was given daily in most public schools of our country. This consisted of exercises given to children standing in the aisles between their desks: rising on heels, turning feet to touch throughout their full length, then toeing out to approximate a forty-five degree angle. In this position directions were followed: to raise arms straight overhead, to front, to sides, and backward, expanding the chest and touching the shoulder blades at the back if possible.

Those children who failed to bring the chest far enough forward or the shoulders far enough back to suit the popular ideas of "proper posture" were fitted with shoulder braces by the parents. These braces were made of broad straps of cotton tape fastened at the back by two metal buckles, with single straps coming over the shoulders, around and under the arms to cross tapes at the back. They were cruel devices to make little children sit up straight at their lessons. To write comfortably at the desk they had to sit sidewise.

In school the daily exercise finished with a grand march around the room. Shoulders and chests were commented on by the teacher and, if criticized, were corrected by the pupils. The constant admonition to toe out was given the children of the Gay Nineties by the teachers and by the parents.

These earnest and well-meaning endeavors of both teachers

and parents to build good physiques and healthy bodies for the children increased the strain of living. Neither orthopedists nor osteopaths had been commonly heard of in those days. Perhaps the very structural maladjustments produced by this persistent training in the wrong direction stimulated these early pioneers of bone adjustment to valuable research in body mechanics.

At that time the "white plague" was engaging the concentrated attention of men of medicine and science. It was thought virtuous by all to *expand the chest* and to do breathing exercises to "strengthen the lungs." The *rest cure* for tuberculosis came later as a result of many years of experiment and study.

Today the effects of those habits of thought, when the chest was stressed for both appearance and for health, still grip the imagination of many. We have ceased to think it a virtue to toe out and even the manuals published by the army no longer insist upon the "forty-five degree angle" in dress parade. Exercises are no longer valued for the "development" of lungs and chest through *forced full breathing*. In these days of high tempo, restful quiet rhythms favoring a relaxed and peaceful body are becoming more highly favored as corrective methods.

FORMS OF EXERCISE

Since the days of Ling, much has been said about exercises both new and old, and much of it might have been left unsaid to no great loss.

We need no more systems to die, as they have lived, in the advertiser's hands. What is needed is a better understanding of the *true mechanics* of the human body.

Forms of exercise may be studied in relation to laws of physics. For example, increase in speed and increase in resistance to movement may be used as means of progression in difficulty.

We all know that swinging the arms rapidly increases the circulation of the blood; that running does the same thing. We are likely to use more energy when pushing somebody as strong or stronger than ourselves than when just pushing a stone wall.

So we may have progression in the form of speed and resistance, or we may produce a progression in exercise by presenting to ourselves other mechanical handicaps. By narrowing our bases or lengthening our levers we bring into play the laws of leverage against gravity and thus increase our struggles. For example, experiment with free arm-swinging and trunk-bending exercise with feet well apart—a very simple exercise. Then bring the feet close together in parallel lines, or heel to toe in a straight line, and the exercise is not quite so easily done. Stand on a rail, heel to toe, and go through the same exercise with the same tension of arms. Try a tightrope, adding a cane to lengthen the leverage. It is plain to see progression in difficulty, also how necessary it is for our various body mechanisms to *prepare* to deal with it.

Any of these forms of progression in exercise may be valuable for those interested in increasing physical prowess. But are they valuable for daily living?

Dr. A. S. Eddington says this in *The Nature of the Physical World:* "When we stand on the ground the molecules of the ground support us by hammering on the soles of our boots with a force equivalent to some ten stone weight. But for this we would sink through the interstices of the floor. We are being continually buffeted."

And so it is a fundamental problem for our living cells to meet the strain of such a bombardment of impulses from the foundation beneath our feet, upon which we ordinarily consider ourselves completely at rest.

Man at all times presents habitual body attitudes, maintaining his own identity. Too many of these are superimposed with no thought of the effect on body functions. Many body attitudes are due, however, to the shape and arrangement of the bones, the adjustable parts of the mechanism, which are continually subjected to the law of gravity and the laws of motion. They help to shape behavior and form a part of the expensive or conservative use of our energy. The economic operation of laws governing our bony framework requires understanding if we desire to aid them intelligently in their work.

Painting, swimming, playing the violin, bringing the golf score under one hundred, are essentially aspects of bodily poise. Maximum improvement results from better balance and coordination of the whole. It never results from cultivating individual muscles or sets of muscles out of proper relation to the other parts of the body. Repetition of specific exercises which may pass for "practice" *rarely forwards* the acquisition of poise and balance, since during the exercise the body retains *all the indoctrinated strains and imperfect adjustments.* It only does, *many times with special emphasis, the wrong thing over and over. Understanding balance, and thinking through the body* should accompany all practice. Muscles and thinking act together in the imagination.

It is out of an imperfect application of the mechanical forces and the emotional desires that the major strains in the human being arise. By understanding them, we can acquire a dynamic balance of our many adjustable parts with the least possible effort. This reduces strain.

SOCIAL CONSCIOUSNESS IN "POSTURE"

Although theoretically the individual is self-sufficient and does not derive his significance merely from his relations with another human being or from groups, actually the *emphasis on "posture" is identified with social consciousness.* This is expressed mostly through the head, shoulders, and chest. The animal, we may recall, uses these parts for alert response and to give direction to his activities; their characteristic use is one of flexible, but directed, expansive action. In modern man, when expansive activities are inhibited, the tensions of alertness are increased and maintained. The head, neck, and chest are stiff.

The cat has acquired no stiffened muscles trying to conform to a social pattern. Neither is she troubled by anxieties as to how to pay her taxes, satisfy her landlord, or provide food and fur for her offspring. She is free from the neuromuscular reflexes of these and similar mental and emotional strains. Her bones are in balance, her muscles unlocked and free, her circulatory mechanisms unimpeded by static, immobile, surrounding tissues. She is ready for instant, competent action. When not in action she can rest, completely relaxed yet in full control of her body. There is no fixity or pose in her primary reflexes. But on the "social animal," fixations are a habit.

Our concept of good body-alignment should be based first on principles of balance applied to the human bony framework; second on recognition of organized preparation for movement inherent in the body mechanisms, and on movement of small parts to make adjustments.

PERSONALITY IN BODY EXPRESSION

Improved bodily alignment is the net result of much that has gone before in our concepts. If one feels a definite moral responsibility to hold certain parts of his body in a fixed position through some "virtuous idea," or if he has a complete lack of responsibility in regard to the arrangement of his units of weight, he has produced fixities in a dynamic structure. Either of these extremes, slumping or bracing, throws greater strain upon certain muscles than upon others and a harmful lack of bone balance follows.

The stooped body, resulting from persistent habits of slumping, is the giving way of individualism to the cosmic forces. The pattern affects the thinking of the individual as well as his appearance, and for the same reason. That is, his nervous and muscular systems give up to outside forces their individual initiative. Cooperation with these forces is lost.

Most persons respond quickly, and with characteristic body attitudes, to such admonitions as "stand straight," "have a stiff backbone," "take it on the chin," "don't carry your wishbone where your backbone ought to be." These expressions are moral interpretations of character. Good morals, perhaps, but bad mechanics. They recondition the postural reflexes by the imposition of artificial, strained positions of parts in relation to the whole. The body, however, would react perfectly to *mechanical facts* if we entertained them in the imagination. If we know where our bones are supported, we can seat them with ease.

Factual information produces sound concepts. These concepts pictured in daily activities facilitate quickened responses. Altering the stimuli will alter the relation of body parts and emotional strains. By substituting nature's laws in our thinking in the place of notions and phobias, we reduce the pressures of emotion and further the coordination of all body parts. The postural reflexes have a significance in the integrity of body systems. William James emphasized the fact that smooth bodily functioning is never possible when there is either emotional or structural distortion.

Movement must be understood in order to secure poise and integration of the personality. Thinking and feeling, muscles and bones, must be given equal responsibility in the economy of the human being. Movement cannot be separated from thinking and emotion. Through muscular action man's bones are kept in balanced adjustment, but he must realize, also, what his inner velocities are doing to him and how his muscles respond to them. A muscle is a dynamic little engine. Its self-generated energy may be wasted or it may be spent with profit. We can determine which.

DIFFICULTIES INHERENT IN THE UPRIGHT POSITION

One of man's greatest difficulties in learning to balance himself successfully on his two upright supports is owing to the way his trunk, at the pelvis, rests on the heads of the thighs. These two slippery balls, perhaps an inch and a half in diameter and seven or eight inches apart, fit into well-lubricated sockets on the *front* side of the pelvis. They form rotary joints and allow movement in *all* directions.

It is a great marvel that we can keep our bodies balanced on these two big smooth "marbles." How this is accomplished has been one of nature's most important secrets. There is no way to escape this necessity and we meet it with varying degrees of dexterity.

Other difficulties that must be understood and met in the biped position is a relatively high center of gravity, a narrow base, small bases of support throughout the body, and finally the need of weight control through a flexible, upright column. In addition to the upright position of this column, its twenty-four separate vertebrae sit on and transfer weight through soft cushions, intervertebral discs, instead of bony platforms, the posterior facets, which formerly supported weight in the four-legged position.

PSYCHOLOGICAL INFLUENCES ON THE UPRIGHT POSITION

In addition to the inherent difficulties of standing erect and of walking freely on two legs, there are plenty of other unfortunate influences which beset us to unbalance our bones as life goes on.

In childhood we are prone to imitate the gait and poses of father or mother, of admired comrade or movie star. The more striking and eccentric these attitudes are, the more likely are they to invite imitation. Such mimicry, made either consciously or unconsciously, may establish lifelong habits of tension and imbalance. There are also various social and psychological influences which may operate in the environment of the growing child to promote emotional strain and unbalanced bodily responses.

A child who is a bit feeble compared to his fellows may be jeered at by brothers and sisters and may develop a sense of inferiority, leading to continued and increased awkwardness. We know that this by no means comes from the humble recognition and acceptance of deficiencies, but rather from a feeling of gross injustice, against which the child revolts. Tensions develop. He responds in various ways. He may acquire a slinking, apologetic, and evasive manner as a result of bashfulness, feeling a lack of sympathy, with consequent social discomfort, or he may deport himself in an aggressive and quite-as-good-as-you-if-not-a-great-deal-better attitude. There are also the docile, who later in life suffer from father's or mother's well-meant but mistaken injunction to "stretch up," to "throw out the chest," or "pull in the chin."

As life goes on we may be seduced by conventional and social "postures." How should a distinguished lawyer, preacher, or surgeon look? How should a fine lady make her appearance? It is common enough to find some hidden ideal of *how we think we should appear* showing itself in artificial body attitudes when meeting the unusual social or business situation. Styles in clothing have a very definite effect on body attitudes and poses. In the days of the bustle people emphasized the high chest, because that increased the "bustle."

Rigidity and slumping involve expensive strains. On the other hand, strain and pomposity may be supplanted by easy, simple grace and dignity. These can be achieved.

Only man has stretched himself out to the surfaces, become surface-minded. His consciousness of how he looks has made harder work of living. "What should my face, my hands, my chest do?" All such questions should be subordinated to the fundamentals of body balance. Balance of bone is the first essential for grace and freedom. Increased sensory appreciation is the second essential. Without sensory appreciation the many small moves necessary for improved bone-relationship are difficult to assemble.

Moralizing or speculating over our body parts frustrates free movement and produces strained, artificial relationships between bony levers and central control. This places handicaps upon coordinating muscles. Our choices must relate to facts. These facts are where and how our bones sit, hang, or are braced. Our muscles will do the rest.

EXAMPLES OF GOOD BALANCE

Most small children are artists in using the body as a unit. Witness the freedom of the whole body in the nursery pillow-fight. The child riding his velocipede, swimming, climbing, is sensitive to all elements in the situation and quickly adjusts himself with mechanical ease to the learning process. When elders moralize with him over the individual parts of his body in terms of "good" or "bad" positions, the full functioning of the child's mechanism is inhibited and his timing system confused. When they encourage the child to "fix" or "hold" parts of his body in particular positions, he loses the freedom which comes through natural spinal control.

The long stealthy stride of the Indian, the child learning his physiological balances in that most difficult of motor skills—walking—these are examples of central control. The low, rolling gait of the peasant carrying a heavy weight on the head or shoulders instinctively follows the pattern of the fighting animal in controlling his weights. The center of gravity is maintained low in the body for ease in carrying the top weights. Also weight is carried more easily on the head or shoulders than in the arms because top weights are managed more easily by a flexible upright than are side weights. As all weights of the body are attached to the spine, *coordinated action of the extremities* through spinal control is a *primary necessity*.

HABITS OF BALANCE

The conscious integration of parts of the body into a well-coordinated unit simply requires the cultivation of thinking about the correct balance of the separate units of weight. These units, balanced at their points of support, facilitate freedom of action. After these habits have been established, the special skills, such as dancing, riding, jumping, or singing, will all be performed with much greater ease because the individual is already habituated to a proper mechanical balance and use of his body and is conscious of the reasons for good balance. Know how your head sits, how your arms and ribs hang, how your pelvis is braced.

Establishing balance at points of support when at rest favors greater freedom and range of movement when expanded action takes place. The nearer to center the parts are supported, the farther they can move away from center in organized movement. Energy is freed for *useful work.* As less is expended in holding unbalanced positions, more is released for movement.

It is safe to say that any bony projection disfiguring the smooth contour of the body wall is caused by an off-center, unbalanced weight. Watch for fixation of any part of your bony skeleton. Hold less, balance more. When you know where the separate units hang, sit, or are braced, you can move them frequently though imperceptibly, with the least possible work of muscles. Keep them close to their supports—close to their centers. Shift positions often.

CHAPTER XII

Man, a Successful Biped

No living creatures except birds and men are successful bipeds. Even man cannot walk when he is born. Children begin usually to go on hands and knees when they are from five months to a year old and continue to do so for about three or four months, when they gradually begin to walk upright in a tottering fashion. As in all other arts, some of us gain a greater proficiency than others. Both standing and walking are only half natural to us. Both are difficult to perfect to the greatest degree of efficiency.

FROM FOUR LEGS TO TWO LEGS

In man's original four-footed position, the bones of the pelvic basin formed an *arch* of which the wedge-shaped sacral bone was the keystone. In the thousands of years since he rose on his hind legs and decided henceforth to be a biped, his bony structure has changed little. When he assumed an erect attitude, he altered the position of his pelvic arch, turning it on its buttressing thighs so that the keystone now appears at the back of the pelvis instead of at the top. The keystone is still firmly braced, however, and still supports weight, though less efficiently than in its four-legged position.

Any structure with four contacts with the earth establishes a body-plane parallel with the ground. It has greater security and stability because of a broad base. A dog or horse on four legs has a greater, safer range of motion than when it is standing on two legs. As the body is lifted and the base is narrowed, the vertical axis of weight transference is less secure and lies in different planes.

It was a slow transition for primitive man to change from the quadruped position with horizontal spine and four supporting uprights into the two-legged vertical position in which the spine no longer served as a cross-girder. At first, squatting was man's normal position; his crouch muscles and ligaments were too closely integrated for him to stand entirely erect. Gradually changes took place, and as he stretched upward his framework suffered maladjustment at its bony joinings. Due to the fact that there was no bone connecting the breast bone with the pelvis rim, the chest was lifted too rapidly and the front of the pelvic scarcely lifted at all. The antagonizing muscles were thrown out of balance for free, opposing functioning; the crouch muscles were weakened through lack of use. Thus the pelvis and thorax were too widely separated in the front, and the visceral organs, instead of being a compact mass, occupied too much space at the front. This caused sagging and bulging of soft tissues in this area of the body and increased the tension of all spinal muscles to hold back the loads tumbling forward. Shearing (sliding) stress was increased between the fifth lumbar vertebra and the sacrum, unbalancing the contact of the spinal column with its base.

Many functional organic ailments, as well as structural maladjustments, of today may be referred to man's struggle to become upright. The perfect mechanical adjustment is not yet attained. A broad base and controlled distribution of weights around the vertical axis establish balance. Shearing must be reduced in all vertebral joints and at the lumbo-sacral joint for the human body to function successfully in this position.

The relationship of parts of the trunk and of basic muscles and joints may be better interpreted by standing on hands and knees, then noting changes when lifting to the upright position. In the four-support position, weight is transferred to the ground through four vertical uprights. The front body-wall from pelvic rim to the "Adam's Apple," and the back body wall from sacrum to skull, are in planes parallel to the ground. The trunk thus is a compact structure with contents neither stretched nor cramped. The sacral keystone of the pelvic arch, the sacroiliac joints, and the buttressing thighs are in the same vertical plane. They are in a right-angle relationship to the horizontal spine and are well integrated with it through the crouch muscles and their fascial structures.

Change in the relative position of the pelvic arch and the buttressing thighs had to occur before man could attain the upright position. If the alignment and compactness of the trunk is maintained the adjustment to the upright must be made at the thigh joints in front, not at the lumbar spine at the waistline in back. If bending takes place here, the abdomen is stretched. Since the thighs must remain vertical for support, the position of the pelvic arch was changed to one more nearly approaching the horizontal. The axes of weight thrust through the pelvic arch thus lay in diagonal lines, from the center top of the sacrum, where the spinal weight is received, to the center of the thigh joints on each side in front. Someplace between these two diagonal lines the center of gravity of the whole must lie.

The pelvis is seen, therefore, to be swinging between two balancing forces—forces acting downward through the spinal column at the back and forces thrusting upward through the thighs at the front. For best balance, the axes of these two forces should meet at the center top of the sacrum, the keystone of the supporting arch. Keep the pelvis swinging; do not fixate. Sit deep in the pelvis.

The first act of movement is tumbling of weights; the second is recovery. There would be no leverage for recovery if the two weight-bearing uprights, the spine and the thigh, were in the same vertical plane. The tumbling would continue like

Humpty Dumpty's. Separate units must move in opposition to
each other for organized movement. To have expanded motion
a "take-off" is necessary. The "springboard" for recovery and
thus organization of *tumbling bony weights* and the human
timing-system must be in quick coordination for man's expanded
movements to be skillful and sure.

THE LOWER LIMBS

There is no fact of greater import than the way our bodies
are balanced on the heads of the thighs. Little progress can be
made in rectifying faulty balance unless we repeatedly "mark,
learn, and inwardly digest" the facts. *The rotary thigh-joint is a
critical point in our bodily economy.* Many go about with a
grotesque misapprehension of the true situation. We are almost
sure to think of the heads of the thighs as being farther apart
than they are. The common idea is of the thigh joints at the
sides of the pelvis instead of *in the front*. Bear in mind that
the thigh joints of every person are but a *hand-span apart*
across the *front of the pelvis*.

Place the finger about a hand-span downward from the top
of the hip bone at the side to find the great trochanter. This is
a protuberance of the thigh bone to which important muscles
are attached—muscles which swing the bone in its socket. If you
first toe in and then toe out, while your fingers are thus placed,
you will feel this projection moving forward and backward
under your fingers. But the *ball-and-socket joint* is a little higher
and three or four inches deeper in toward the front than the
great trochanter. It is important to realize that this is *where
the leg begins,* also that the round head of the thigh moves *in
all directions* in its well-lubricated socket.

The lower end of the thigh bone expands so as to form the
upper part of the knee joint, the largest joint in the body. Both
its sides can be easily felt.

Below the knee joint are two long bones. The larger is the
shin bone, the *tibia*. Its sharp outer face is easily seen, for it
is ill protected and often gets "barked" in childhood. It is one

of the bones easiest to trace from top to bottom. It receives all the weight of the upper body. The smaller leg-bone laced to it is the *fibula.*

The word *fibula* means "brooch" in classical Latin. The Romans, remember, fastened their togas with a fibula pin, a very ancient device with which we became acquainted in early infancy. The fibula fits to the tibia much as the pin of the safety pin does to its other side.

It is the tibia, not the fibula, that receives the weight of the body at the knee and transfers it to the ankle. The fibula is bound tightly to the side of the tibia by stout ligaments and an interlacing membrane between the bones. Without this type of construction the side stresses which must be borne by the leg, when the foot slips or the body is jarred sidewise, could not be absorbed.

The lower ends of both tibia and fibula are prominent on each side of the ankle, and can be felt as the inner and outer ankle-bones. The tibial prominence is on the inside; the fibular is on the outside.

ANKLE AND FOOT

The fact that weight is transmitted to the foot, where motion and adaptability are required, as well as support for a relatively heavy load, necessitates an extremely strong and flexible mechanism. This the archlike structure of the foot provides.

The tibia, articulating with the foot at the *talus*—the base bone supporting weight—helps to form the ankle joint. The ankle joint acts as a hinge, though slight lateral motion is allowed. The tibia and fibula grasp the talus very much as ice tongs grip a block of ice.

The ankle joint is at the top of an arch whose supporting structure must extend as far behind as in front of the thrust of weight from the tibia at the top. This is essential to give security of weight support to the keystone, the talus.

The talus is the keystone of the arch which is formed by the many bones of the foot. It is held in place by pressure from

adjoined bones and short ligamentous fibers, which attach it to
all the bones abutting it. It is a true keystone, having no tendons
or muscles attached to it. It thus serves as a wedge.

The talus rests on the heel bone, the *calcaneus,* which is
the largest bone of the foot. Extending to the back, it forms one
side of the arch. At the front, it forms only a part of the front
side of the arch. The remainder is formed by four small bones
abutting it.

Seven bones (irregularly shaped blocks bound together by
tough ligaments) form the essential weight-bearing part of the
foot. It is a perfect arch and its balanced forces, one half behind
the contact with the weight-bearing tibia resting upon it and
one half in front, keep its talus keystone in place and offer
security and balance to the weight coming down upon it. This
arch—the *tarsus* of the foot—is sometimes referred to as the
longitudinal arch.

Radiating from the tarsus in the front are five long, slender
bones called the *metatarsals.* Attached to these are the phalanges
of the five toes, two in the big toe and three in each of the
others. These have many short, stout muscles attached, and
serve to counter the thrust of weight from above coming through
the bones of the arch. They must be free and active for this
purpose. Wiggle your toes frequently to insure this freedom.

This extremely brief description barely indicates the intricate structure of our foot, by which twenty-six small bones are
enabled, not only to support our weight but, by means of
muscles, to move it about with swiftness and assurance. Small
wonder that aching feet often disturb our peace of mind. It has
been said that many an important international problem has
failed of solution by some of our top diplomats because of aching feet, with consequent distraction and lowering of spirits.

At the ankle joint, motion is quite free forward and backward but, unlike the thigh joints above, the ankle joints are
strictly limited in sideways motion by the inner and outer
ankle-bones. It is this formation that prevents sidewise shearing
or slipping at the ankle. All weight passes directly to the talus
under the tibia, whence it is distributed to the remaining twenty-

five bones of the foot. These are arranged in a series of arches, of which the longitudinal arch is the most important. All are laced together by stout ties of ligaments and cartilages, like the trussing of a bridge or trestle.

Mechanically, the work of the lower legs is to carry the weight from the base of the trunk to the ground. This must be done in such a way that the back thrust from the ground will be directed in a manner to communicate the least amount of shock to the body. This result is accomplished by the substance, shape, and number of parts, which are characterized by strong elastic tissues and curved, arched, and radial bony structures. Proper balance of these parts acts as an effective shock-absorber.

The success of man as a biped is evidenced not only by his ability to survive but also by his ability to explore his world. He is still proving his success as he continues to explore worlds beyond his known horizons.

CHAPTER XIII

How We Became What We Are

The specific characteristics which make you an individual and me an individual are found in the development and behavior of something so tiny that many thousands, possibly millions, could snuggle together under the head of a pin. These minute bits of living matter, called *genes,* hold the key which unlocks the mysteries by which the character of every living organism in the world is determined. The genes of man determine whether he will be short or tall, blond or brunette, genius or moron.

It is impossible for even the most advanced scientist to tell by examining these genes just what type of person will finally evolve, even impossible to tell whether the resultant organism will be fish, horse, or man. But the genes themselves know the answer. They determine that man always becomes man, and not a lion or an oak tree; that a rose always becomes a rose, not a violet, and that never by any chance does a horse become a dog. So every plant and animal evolving from the living cell carries in its developing nucleus and protoplasm all the potentialities of its species, and of individual characteristics, all the hereditary factors for developing hereditary traits.

The genes make up an exceedingly complex system. Each

gene has a particular function to perform in determining the makeup of the new organism. Every human being is a product of the special arrangement of these genes. If the mother of every person living today had conceived one month earlier or one month later, the individual as he looks, acts, and feels today would never have been born. The world would have been inhabited by an entirely different set of persons.

HEREDITY AND ENVIRONMENT

Every living being represents a combination of one set of genes from the mother and one set from the father. In particular individuals the influence for certain abilities or defects may be recognized as hereditarian, or environmental, or both. If we are to take conscious control of our further evolution we shall need to understand these two forces, namely, heredity and environment. To ascribe to either force a predominant influence in all cases is a mistake.

Professor H. S. Jennings clearly states the modern scientific view: "Which is more important for the characteristics of the organism, heredity or environment? Which is more important for the characteristics of man? Which is more important for the manufacture of automobiles, the materials of which they are made or the method of manufacture? This question is like the other. No single general answer can be given to either. For good results, both fit materials and appropriate treatment of materials are required. From materials of a particular sort, a good machine of one kind can be made, not of another kind. A method of manufacture that will fit one type of material fails with another. Materials that are excellent for one sort of machine are poor for another; and the fittest of materials require proper handling if their possibilities are to be realized. Either poor materials or poor handling can ruin a machine or an organism."

The genes determine our heredity. What we do with that heredity is determined by our environment.

To the uninformed in biology and embryology, this cellular process and development of the genes is not startling, but taken for granted. A cat gives birth to kittens. We expect this to happen, even as we assume that the sun will open our day each morning. But to those who have studied cell division—*mitosis*—these mysteries are a constant wonder. Each individual is a replica of his species and race.

INDIVIDUAL ACTIVITY IN A UNITED WHOLE

After the combining of the genes from both father and mother (one half taken from each so that the new entity will not be overloaded with twice the number of characteristics of the father and the mother) the living cell begins its most intricate and interesting process of subdivision. A multicellular structure results. Not really a new life, but life carried forward in common by two, living, microscopic cells! Union, reproduction: one and the same thing!

The individual entities *combine* in the same way as in a chemical compound the *primary elements combine* to form a new compound, each new compound having individual and specific characteristics entirely different from those of the original elements. For example, the solid chemical element, sodium, explodes when placed in water, burns human skin, and catches fire in the air. Chlorine, greenish yellow in color, is a deadly poisonous war-gas. Yet when sodium and chlorine combine they produce common salt, without which our bodies could not live. So we see that the new formation is not merely the addition of the parts. It has new qualities through the organization of the parts into a whole. It is a creative synthesis. In similar manner the combining elements of the two living cells produce a creative synthesis, *not addition, but integration.* The human germ cells, after this integration, proceed to divide into a multicellular structure. Soon the two cells are four, the four are eight, the eight are sixteen; then in rapid and orderly series the cell mass increases until the cells begin to assume appearances that differentiate them. The little genes are already projecting their determinant qualities into the forming of this new entity.

THE THREE PRIMARY LAYERS

Cell division is still a deep mystery, even though the minute processes may be observed. This process in the evolution of cell division is highly selective. Some cells form an outer layer of the mass quite separate and distinct from the inner and middle layers. The embryologist tells us that this outer layer, the *ectoderm,* forms the skin, hair, nails, and nervous systems; the middle layer, the *mesoderm,* gives rise to the circulatory, skeletal, and muscular systems; the inner layer, the *endoderm,* develops into the respiratory and digestive systems. These three highly specialized parts of the embryo are called the three primary layers. Out of them comes all that we are.

THE MOVING FORCES OF OUR ORGANISM

The original cells now change to meet the needs of a developing organism. The three primary layers have the wisdom to build and develop the most amazing and intricate mechanism in the world, that of the living being, and at the same time build organisms to generate its driving power.

What chemical or physical force in the cells of the mesoderm drives them to develop contractile substances and qualities such as we find, for instance, in the muscles of the body? How do the cells of the outer layer know when and in what manner to fold upon themselves to begin the production of the spinal cord? What guiding force urges them through the maze of development to produce ultimately a whole set of such diverse parts? Little light could be thrown upon these questions if nothing were known of simpler forms of life.

The single-celled creatures, the simplest form of life, have a nucleus corresponding in function to our brain and nervous system. It reacts to stimuli, it assimilates its food, disposes of waste, and reproduces by cell division. All this may be observed under a microscope. It is a very busy little creature on its own plane.

INHERITED HABITS

The forces operating in our various cells are the inherited habits of protoplasm—namely, the spiritual, chemical, and physical forces in the cells that enabled, through millions of years, the ancestors of these cells to meet the life situations with which they were faced. The living stream of energy flows on.

The mechanisms of heredity contained in the germ cells lead us to this important question—is there anything that human intelligence can do to guide human evolution? Could we make it impossible in the future for a poet to lament in the spirit of Wordsworth, "and much it grieves my heart to think what man has made of man"?

We find in the orderly arrangement of living cells the basis for even the highest manifestations of human behavior. The cells are responsible for high resolves, the great motives that drive men to action, and, what is still more marvelous, they furnish the power to carry out that action.

These myriad, microscopic units have been building throughout the long years of evolution and have produced man as he is. Not only the living body has resulted, but *functional capabilities* in a wide variety of form, culminating in the intricate and finely coordinated function of thinking, leading man on to ever-higher aspirations of attainment. Inner forces have balanced with outer forces and developed cells and systems adequate for survival of the organism as a whole. A complete unit! A unit of purpose and organization!

ADHERENCE TO TYPE

The functions that the cells and various systems develop are resident within their protoplasms. Certain ones can no more refrain from forming bones than others can avoid the necessity to produce blood. This nature of cells to pursue the path laid out for them in the inherited germ plasm of the race is subject to variations according to certain chemical and biological laws, as we observe in the necessity for typing blood. But there appears to be no reason, other than an inexorable ancestry, to explain their adherence to type. Millions of years of practice make them what they are.

The chemical elements found in the human cell are carbon, hydrogen, oxygen, nitrogen, sulphur, phosphorus, magnesium, calcium, potassium, and iron. These are called the base metals of the body. A proper balance of these metals is essential for our good health. These primary elements present in the human cell are found only in animal and plant life. The same type of cell structure appears in the living stuff of plants and animals, and it may even be difficult to differentiate between them, although there is a great diversity in the manner of functioning in the various types of organisms.

An animal takes protoplasm—the matrix of living cells—ready-made from other animals or from plants. A plant, on the other hand, can transform carbonic acid, water, and ammonia into *living substance*. Plants grow and reproduce but they do not move about in the purposeful activity of animals. Plants accumulate power; animals utilize and distribute it.

There are, in addition to our base metals, other compounds necessary to the life of man, which are formed *only by living plant-cells*. These are carbohydrates, sugar, and starch. The vegetable fats, oils, and proteins compounded by living plant cells are also important to the well-being of man. The examination of the chemical behavior of "matter," both organic and inorganic, is a science in itself, however, and we cannot expound it here. Suffice it to say that these physico-chemical organisms are struggling to maintain balance by replacement and rearrangement of their separate parts in the continuous cycle of metabolism—the process of burning, refueling, and burning again.

THE MOST IMPORTANT CHEMICAL REACTION IN THE WORLD

"Photosynthesis" has been called the "most important chemical reaction in the world." The product of this life-building reaction is called chlorophyll. It is the green coloring-matter in plants. Upon its agency the very life of the living cell depends. The interesting fact about this synthesis is that it must take place in the presence of light—hence its name: photosynthesis.

And so we find that every living plant has an original creative process which no living creature can duplicate. In its protoplasm it creates a necessary ingredient for the life of man. We may more fully realize the *intelligence* which lies hidden in this chemical birth if we watch the student in the chemical laboratory as he applies heat or cold, force or pressure, to the primary elements in his test tubes out of which he builds his new compounds. He must *know the rules* discovered by men who have devoted their lives to chemical science or he could never know what elements have affinity for each other and in what proportions they will act favorably. When shall he apply the flame, the centrifuge? The rules of his game are the laws of chemistry.

Due to the important reaction called photosynthesis we have in the humble dandelion, in alfalfa, and in other living plants agents of chemistry so intelligent that they can take minerals (primary elements) out of the ground and so mix them in their own protoplasm with the rays of the sun that a new and vital chemical birth takes place. Chlorophyll is born! *And you may live because of it!*

Our need for these elements of chemical origin requires that we should eat plenty of green plants and vegetables grown above ground. The sun has added something invaluable to their chemical composition. How many millions of years did it require in the evolution of the cosmos for this essential creative act to perfect itself? How many millions of years is God's "First Day," His "Second Day," His "Third Day"?

MAN'S BIOLOGICAL BEHAVIOR

The biological forces in the organism are obviously complex. Living substances form an integrated organism, the very process of whose integration develops the individual. Examples

of this are numerous in various forms of life. Witness the cater-
pillar forming the butterfly, related to its ancestor, the worm;
the gill-slits or arches appearing in the human embryo, recalling
man's aquatic ancestry. Our cells still live in an aquarium. We
are very wet indeed as soon as we get under the skin. The salty
body fluids are essential to the life and balance of the body cell.

We cannot further elaborate here the biochemical elements
of living substance. The subject would fill a volume by itself.
We wish merely to stimulate the imagination to appreciate the
dynamic quality of the internal phenomena of living cells as
they struggle incessantly for equilibrium to serve our purposes.
In these living units we have the complete history of physical
life.

If, as seems probable, life has existed upon the earth for
five hundred million years, the succession of living things in
the series leading up to man are like a string of peas in a pod,
or fruit on a tree, each individual having the power to continue
the series. The oak lies in the acorn, the onion in the seedling,
man in the ovum. Life comes only from life. The race and
species thus extend themselves in a living flow of energy.

In the cellular sense, man's destiny is in the activity of his
cells. The regulation of cellular activity in regard to aspects
of the environment is seen in the cellular changes manifesting
themselves in dealing with food, heat, moisture in the air, air
movement, and clothing. The effects of cellular changes often
rise into consciousness, bringing feelings of comfort or discomfort, pain or pleasure, and we make appropriate adjustments.

FACING FACTS

As science replaces sentimentality in social affairs there will
be less radical behaviorism that denies the importance of inheritance, and less of hereditarian snobbery that looks to "blood"
for everything.

The study of man's behavior must begin with human nature
as it is and with the world as we find it. Before man can take
conscious control of his development, he must acquire knowl-

edge of the mechanical and chemical problems of a living organism, and must rid himself of a host of superstitions, fears, prejudices, and despairs that now weigh him down. Unless he can master these, he still remains, so far as his own life is concerned, in the Dark Ages. The two great tangible influences in the life of man, the biological and the social, beat upon him from the moment of cell fertilization until his exit from the stage of life. Thus man is the product of two forces—the genes of the germ plasm from which he comes and the influence of the environment in which he develops. Both his ancestors and his immediate family influence this product.

The individual organism is one in a long series of generations, and with a varying success in adaptation. Some adapt so poorly that they never fully live—they merely exist, full of discomforts and self-accusations. They understand neither the true nature of their substance and environment nor the facts relating to themselves and to their objective behavior.

OUR TWO PASTS

The child, from the moment he becomes an individual organism, is a slave to two pasts, each demanding that its importance be fully considered, leading him to different goals, to different actions. One is what he is by nature; the other, what history and society have made of him by customs and beliefs. Being an infant in a home dominated by social demands—and whose is not?—he must be clothed to satisfy his mother's pride, when by nature he wishes only to eat and sleep.

Our biological and historial pasts are ever at war with each other, although there are parts of *both* that are important to a prolonged civilization. Virtue lies in selection, not in inhibition. Blending seems impossible, but choices may be made and balances struck.

The child's two pasts begin to travel separate ways almost as soon as he looks out upon his world and feels the urge of the many little egos within, clamoring to express life. And here he meets the beginning of controls, those crystalized patterns of thought and behavior developed through man's evolution toward civilization. His way is too often darkened by shadows of bygone prejudices and phobias still largely controlling the present environment in which he is forced to live. The social past has brought to him some necessary inhibitions which enable him to live with his fellows in an organized society; but also there are many which are unnecessary strains upon him.

The great movement of humankind in a restless endeavor to find life that sustains or power that controls is evidence of *dynamic man in response to the forces that play upon him,* rather than an argument for progress, ultimate or not. In the valley civilizations of four great rivers, the Nile, the Hwang Ho, the Ganges, and the Tigris-Euphrates, kings rose and religious leaders ascended to power and successfully promoted all kinds of fears, established various traditions and enacted codes of behavior that favored perpetuation of the ruling class. Education was not considered conducive to submissiveness, hence for thousands of years the masses were kept in ignorance and fear. Told and retold from generation to generation are man's beliefs and interpretations of life for many thousands of years. These still form a background in our memory.

CONTRIBUTIONS OF THE GREEKS AND ROMANS

The spirit of democracy was born in Greece, and civilization there rose to a height unsurpassed. Intellectual development was an aspiration. Observation of nature's behavior, both in the universe and in man, held a deep interest.

The early Greeks produced the "Golden Age" of art and physical perfection, as well as philosophies influencing man's behavior and thinking. Harmony and beauty controlled their thought. Their growth lay in the simplicity of their belief and response to the discoveries of their intellectual leaders. The "Golden Age" of Pericles and Euclid has never been surpassed. We are still striving to master the dynamic symmetry lying hidden in the marble and clay of the age of Pericles.

As the philosophies and art of Greece have influenced

thinking and feeling throughout the ages, so the development of law—the code of behavior—has come down to us from the statesmen of ancient Rome. The august names of the Caesars spring to us from the pages of that distant past.

In the Roman period of expansion, however, much of the truth and art gleaned from the Greek civilization was lost. The fighting Romans created demands for the development of muscle, rather than for harmony and balance. Military systems valued bodily exercises for their utilitarian effects; for their ability to mold the individual into a capable soldier. Man was taught to become more efficient in killing man. Physical pleasures, big chests, bulging muscles were the keys to success.

THE REACTION OF THE EARLY CHRISTIANS

Early Christians took quite the opposite view of life and associated the idea of earthly pleasure with that of vice, concluding that suffering was, in itself, a virtue. Thus was born the philosophy of asceticism. The *mind* or spirit was considered essentially divine and pure, while evil was inherent in matter. Could man but be freed from that hampering sack of bones, blood, and muscles, the *soul* could soar to great heights!

The Renaissance saw a revival of the values of early Greek and Roman learning and civilization. There was new interest in the human being. Hygiene and physical exercise again received notice from a populace tired of subordinating and punishing the body. The desire to enjoy life led to the desire to understand it. Even Martin Luther advocated physical education as a preventive of vice.

THE SOCIAL PAST

Added to the moral and religious past is the traditional social past of the individual stylists and faddists. They, too, have set their mark upon the behavior of man, with the military high chest, the turned-out toes, the Grecian bend, the debutante slouch. The effect of many of these notions may still be seen in our fashion plates of today.

In all groups of society the remote past with its picturesque "fairy tales," artificial values which emphasize the transient rather than the important characteristic, has brought countless unthinking persons to curious beliefs, unnatural bodily attitudes, and ridiculous speech.

Man's past cannot be obliterated. He cannot escape the smallest part of that which has gone before in his social and biological history. The past that he drags after him, the past that clings to him as closely as a shadow and yet more solidly than matter itself, is incorporated in his flesh and bones, his spinal cord, his muscles, brain, and numerous glands. These have been fashioned by time and by use, developed and perfected through the millions of yesterdays that stretch uncounted back into the beginning of all things.

CHAPTER XIV

Adaptation to Environment

You can catch a glimpse of the most ancient way of life, in which mere awareness seems at times to be intelligence, by dipping up a little ditch-water on which a scum has collected. One drop of this placed upon a microscope slide under a cover-glass, and magnified about six hundred diameters, will look as if it were a whole lake swarming with life, both animal and plant. The animals dart and twist about, expand and contract in such a bewildering way that it is impossible, without pro-longed study, to determine how they are formed. Some of them move slowly, as do many of the plants. The various groups differ greatly in their forms and habits.

Two students observing these groups through the same microscope came upon a lachrymaria, a single-celled creature which is supposed to look like a Roman tear-jar, hence its name. It can thrust out a threadlike "neck," twenty times the length of its body. This it swings about in every direction, with an incessant rhythmic movement, seeking food. One specimen happened to tie a knot in its "neck" and, instead of reeling it in, the creature stopped all activity so quickly that it did not even tighten the loop. After this apparent "appraisal," it quickly flowed its body through the loop and was on the job again. This action reveals a high degree of awareness as well as the ability to make an adequate response. That was a life-saving situation.

If you view through a microscope myriads of these tiny single-celled creatures you will observe that they act as though theirs were the only sphere of activity, and their urge all there were to life. The same could be observed in an ant colony or a beehive. Even human beings sometimes act as though they believed the same of themselves. If a telescope could be turned upon us from a remote planet, how would our mad rush seem to those living there? We might appear to be just flying about with no apparent purpose.

Living things show development from one physical plane to another. Activity and movement are continuous on all planes of life, and the activities of those in each plane seem more or less innocent of purpose to those above or below it, yet all movement is purposive. Would it not be wise for us, if and when possible, to observe life closely on as many planes as we can for saner appraisal of all? Knowledge of the natural sciences tends to reduce egotism.

THE EGOCENTRIC

Because of exaggerated self-importance, many of us have no desire to learn more facts even on our own plane. The expression of life nearest us we too often take for granted. Each one lives unto himself alone and his drives and competencies have been developed from earliest childhood in self-consciousness. Stretching the imagination into other fields is necessary to enlarge our vision. If we absorb more of the knowledge at hand we might crack our egos and determine what lies behind our own egotism.

We all wear blinders. The more egocentric the person, the tighter the blinders fit! Throw the blinders aside and turn your microscope upon other subjects and human beings at your side as you would study the ants and bees, the stentors, the lachrymarias, and the amoebae. Learn more of the behavior of forces and the expressions of energy in other individual entities, both animate and inanimate. This will enable you to understand a greater number of the deep causes for your own behavior. Then turn the microscope upon yourself.

There are no "good" or "bad" habits handed on by the genes, only potentialities for negative or positive use of human qualities. By reason and intelligence, or by neglect, environment may do much to make or break the balance in personality. Your basic nature, that given you by the genes, cannot be changed, but its *character-forces* can be guided. Learn what your inherent qualities are. Accept them, respect them, and, through guidance and action, build them into a constructive personality. This is possible and not too difficult when proper intelligence is applied. Accept yourself. The acceptance of self would be easier if we understood that there is a common ground of behavior for all living beings.

After you have created your inner environment through your imagination your *truthful adjustment to yourself* must come before you can adjust fearlessly to your environment. If you do not use your imagination constructively, it will be shadowed by self-pity, a combination of fear and self-indulgence. Here lies the root of maladjustment. The moving currents of your body are emotional, and these must be truthfully interpreted and guided by clearer thinking about them.

Build your basic nature and others will have respect for it. In youth, you may have decided that it wasn't "worth the bother," but in later life, you *revamp your thinking*. It is never too late to create a new environment and expand a personality. Entertain facts in the imagination. Through the imagination only living becomes real, affecting both the inner and outer balances.

CONTINUITY OF TYPE

How the "chromosomes" (containing the genes) persist in their conformity to type is one of the great secrets of the universe. The continuity of type, the persistency of species in plant and animal, and the survival urge is inherent in all living things.

The individual chemical laboratories in plant life continue to work out their specific formulae. Their chemical composition determining physical growth makes them what they are. Flowers, vegetables, trees never mistake their own specific survival urge for that of another; the oak is always an oak, the rose a rose.

Were it not for the persistency of this survival urge in the various forms of plant life, man could not survive. In these chemical laboratories the primary elements of both poisons and safe foods lie in adjacent territory, but the spinning thread of survival keeps the species clear. Man knows where to find his safe food and can avoid that which is dangerous to him. Undomesticated animals instinctively swerve from foods not meant for them. The survival urge is God's way of keeping the earth populated.

TOOLS FOR SURVIVAL

Many unseen mechanisms are worked out in all forms of life to serve as means for survival. In the living animal, hunger and sex are the most important of these. Fear and rage are tools in the service of these two. In the stimuli and response system we find the mechanism for emotion, and thinking is the tool developed in its service.

The extent to which the whole organism is involved in all behavior problems is indicated by James's observation: "One's ethical judgments may be determined as much by one's circulation as by logical grounds." Life is safeguarded by this view because we now see the organism as susceptible to change.

INCESSANT COORDINATION

Standing, sitting, and lying still are merely relative forms of expression. The body is never still, awake or asleep. The heart must always be throbbing, about once a second, sending throughout the arteries and capillaries a stream of blood, which finds itself back to the heart, by way of the veins, in an incredibly short time. The ribs and diaphragm must always be moving, to draw in oxygen and expel carbon dioxide. The lungs must be exchanging these gases, the stomach squeezing and churning, and the intestines writhing. All these are but gross and obvious actions. Besides these, the salivary glands, gastric glands, pancreas, and liver must be forming chemical combinations at the right moment for organic balance. Our hydraulic pressure must be kept constant to meet the atmospheric pressure of fifteen pounds to the square inch of body surface. Our body temperature must be kept constant in spite of sudden changes in outside conditions. In response to the environment, to thinking, and to the activity of the ductless glands, the body is reacting through the neuromusculature, consciously or unconsciously, with ceaseless energy.

The nervous system, with its billions of generating cells and "conducting wires," and as many more responding cells in the nerve centers and sensitive muscle-fibers, constitutes the reacting agents of the human organism for movement. These movements are regulated and tempered, however, by other physiological agents, the ductless glands, and the determinations originating in the frontal brain-cells.

Our receiving and responding mechanisms lie in the nerves, muscles, and glands of the body. But without an arrangement of bones and ligaments conforming to good architectural design, no organized movement could take place. Remember, when we move, we move bones; we do not consciously move muscles. It is movement that resides in the thinking, not muscle action.

The primary and conditioned reflexes, the cortical determinations, and the ductless glands form the automatic mechanisms acting upon the framework of bones and ligaments to effect organized movement in response to awareness of environmental needs.

INFLUENCE OF MODERN LIFE ON SENSORY REPORTS

Modern life tends to restrict unduly the sensory areas. For example, the chemist tests combinations of chemical elements which will further his discoveries in research. His observations are exceptionally keen in this field. When engaged in thoughts of laboratory procedure, he pays scant attention to musical sounds or colors in sunsets. On the other hand, musicians, painters, and sculptors usually take slight interest in the analysis of water or the chemical constituents of the air they breathe. So the necessities of an occupation tend to narrow the range of individual response. The net result of this, of course, is a constriction of the sensory field. By experience and habit the organism tends to receive but a few of the sensory stimuli, so that in time the individual becomes atrophied in a wide range of response.

Age may be reckoned more in terms of the degree of sensitiveness to a wide sensory field than to the passing of years or mere chronology. To keep young, one must keep the receptor doors open to an extended variety of interests. Nothing is clearer in those who have prematurely aged than the narrowness of their interests, the small focus on one bit of life.

Obviously one cannot have a highly developed sensitivity to *all* stimuli in *all* fields. There must be selections regardless of how desirable a great variety might be. Understanding our sensory organism is necessary if wise choices are to be made. One likes to choose between experiences that strengthen and those that weaken, between areas of reception that stimulate a high level of cellular activity and those that enervate.

KINESTHESIA

The kinesthetic sense is a special sense which brings the organism into close relation to its own structural framework, muscles, and joints, and their relationship with the outer world. It is the sum total of sensations conveyed to the brain by sensory nerves from muscles, tendons, and joints—all serving the organization of response.

Through kinesthesia man reacts to his world. As music is the reaction through sound, and painting through color and form, this also is a medium which cannot be quite translated into words. It is joint sensations, muscle sensations, sense of relationship of parts, of one unit to another or of parts of these units to each other. It must be experienced inside the body. Helen Keller, who can neither hear nor see, is the proof that kinesthesia is also a way of life. The meaning of the kinesthetic sense should be carefully reviewed if we are to understand clearly the organization, in the unconscious, of man's behavior. Its responses make possible the numerous activities, modes of expression which are one's *psychic and muscular responses* to life.

In negative thinking-habits, the awareness of resistance to movement, weight pressure, and other discomforts of small parts received in the inner mechanisms form undoubtedly a large share of the self-doubting and discomfort which habituate this type of thinking and make it difficult to change. We remain blind to the real causes and moralize over causes which do not exist—except in fancy. There are remedies, but we must find them in the same organisms that produced the original discomforts.

EVIDENCES OF THE KINESTHETIC PROCESS

The nature of the kinesthetic process may be seen by an analysis of the way in which we become aware of the distance of objects. We are able to say that a table is four feet away, or a piano ten feet, not, as one might suppose, by a special quality of vision or of a specific reaction to light, but chiefly by means of the muscular sense.

The ability to judge distances is built up from a multitude of impressions conveyed from the eye muscles as they focus the visual image upon the retina of the eye. The degree of muscular adjustment necessary varies with the distance, size, and shape of the object observed. Impressions of the work done by the eye muscles are reported to the brain where they are interpreted as indicating a certain distance in space. This interpretation in turn is effected through an association of ideas and memories of various cumulative experiences of the muscles. It takes the baby many months to acquaint himself enough with space to enable him to reach for and grasp the objects of his desire.

Memories of former experiences, movements of the eye, movements of the body in going toward and reaching objects, together with tactile impressions of their shape, extent or size, and texture aid in this interpretation. This spatial perception built up from past experience of body muscles in conjunction with adjusting of the eye muscles is remembered. If this were not so we could not distinguish between a large table ten feet away and a smaller one five feet away, since the visual image and the amount of work done by the eye muscles might be identical.

Through kinesthesia a nicety of adjustment and recognition of slight movements develop. By this aid one is able to estimate the power, distance, and span of movements required in such acts as lifting weights, climbing stairs, throwing balls, or jumping rope. After due preparations are made, the muscular reactions are automatic.

You do not measure the number of pounds that you are about to lift, or count the number of stairs you are about to climb, before you adjust the forces needed; nor do you measure the distance of the rope from the floor before you jump over it, nor apply a yardstick to the field before you throw a ball. These responses are all organized out of past experience.

The sensory reports activate muscles, and muscles move bony levers in orderly fashion according to mechanical laws of leverage and weight transference. To think straighter and throw a straighter ball one must know more of the fundamental principles upon which these operations are based. Through more knowledge one may facilitate freedom, economy of effort, and speedier response in motion. These accurate and intricate regulations are made *below the threshold of consciousness* and are established through the development of the conditioned reflexes.

FAITH AND THE IMAGINATION

In everyday activities we see a thing as *being done* in our imagination, and everything falls into line. All the mechanisms habituated to bodily response in time-space-movement organize and carry through the action. We accomplish without question, without doubt. But were we to insist upon saying, "I can't see myself doing that," this negative attitude would also involve an appropriate response—one of *confused* coordination of the inner mechanisms. Optimism versus pessimism, faith versus doubt—results we have all witnessed!

If we knew more of the possible imbalances involved in living, we would see more clearly how every cell of the body has been nurtured in faith. In all our daily activities we express this profound faith with no realization of it. We know that we can run, climb stairs, swim, drive a car, eat and talk at the same time, and we rarely question these activities, or ask how they are performed. Faith is the prerequisite to all these habituations, and we must learn to carry this degree of faith forward into our new learnings. *See how each thing is being done. And expect it to be done.* Have faith in your imagination and in your mechanisms that have been prepared over lo, these many years, to carry out the activities organized in your imagination. "Faith is the substance of things hoped for, the evidence of things not seen." Through the techniques of imagery, supported by their ally, faith, a confidence is unconsciously established that all desired movement will carry through. We are imbued with an abounding and abiding faith.

THE INTEGRITY OF THE SENSE ORGANS

For eons of time the first essential of life has been its preservation. The drive for action must always be forward—either to fight or to run. Thus the animal survived. Backing up, retreating, was out of the question. The integrity of the sense organs was a prime necessity for this survival. This is aptly illustrated in our woodsmen, and in the native guides employed by our army in the South Pacific during the last war.

Man must now regain his primitive awareness in a *cellular* sense to enable him to be more aware in a cerebral sense. Thus brain, nerves, and muscles will act together to improve our coordination in all that we do or think. We will then think straight ahead and respond intelligently. There will result better organization of movement in the imagination. Imagination will assume its original role in the learning process.

Sensations affecting our decisions and our every act are bombarding us on all sides, although we are often unconscious of the impact of many of them. They are of all kinds, simple, compound and complex, agreeable or disagreeable, welcome or unwelcome. We cannot escape them night or day. They are the stuff out of which our feelings, our conduct, our character, and our destinies are built. They mirror our biological and social pasts as well as our present environment and choices.

These reports are major factors in every life, coming as they do not only from without but from within. The psychologists call them stimuli and, if we think of them in terms of our newer knowledge, we will recognize them for what they actually are, namely, forces which are playing both in and through the mechanisms of which our physical bodies are composed.

EXPEDIENCY

The building of the unseen tools for survival is evident in the very earliest and simplest forms of life, as we may note in the single-celled creature. An interesting instance of appropriate response seen through the microscope is told by Professor H. S. Jennings, who describes the conduct of a species of stentor, which looks a little like a cornucopia. "It has a 'foot' which it attaches to some bit of debris, and then builds a little fortification about itself into which it can withdraw. Around what we might be tempted to call its mouth is a thick-set ring of short hairs (cilia). These look like a revolving wheel when the stentor uses them to sweep in his food from the surrounding water. The movement can be reversed to throw out anything which disturbs the 'animal.' "

Professor Jennings squirted some particles of carmine under the cover-glass. When they reached the stentor it first reversed the movement of its cilia "wheel," which would tend to expel them. Being unsuccessful in this, it then snapped back into its protective tube. In a short time it emerged tentatively, but withdrew again as it came in contact with the carmine. After several trials it broke up its fortress, detached its "foot," and swam away. We cannot call this "intelligent" conduct, for in *our* sense the animal did not *know* what it was doing. It was, however, *expedient* action, which is characteristic of the "wisdom of the body." It is upon this kind of wisdom that man, even today, still must rely.

The tale as told by Professor Jennings is quite exciting. He concluded that "the reaction to any given stimulus is modified by the past experience of the animal, and the modifications are regulatory, not haphazard in character. The phenomena are thus similar to those shown in the 'learning' of higher organisms, save that the modifications depend upon less complex relations and last a shorter time."

We usually greatly exaggerate the number of our voluntary actions compared with those of which we are aware only in the sense that the stentor is aware. The stentor acts intelligently, from our standpoint, but does not realize what it is doing. Our bodily operations also are *to an overwhelming extent performed unconsciously.*

CHAPTER XV

The Conscious and the Unconscious

Activity with devotion to many interests characterizes man at his prime. Life's forces are kept high when reactions are many and varied, and with unselfish interests. Use, not disuse, holds vitality.

The difference between age and youth is the difference in the spirit of adventure which, in terms of daily living, means welcoming change. Life's satisfactions are to be found by determining the directions and guiding the velocities of our own vital energies. Daily choices and actions determine the outcome. Future responses are born of these habits through the unconscious.

The unconscious is not a mystical kind of demon. It's all those things we have forgotten; it's all the things we have grown used to and that are always "coming on." If we have formed the habit of holding our knees strained, our jaws set, we have become unconscious of it. If we have continually resisted our environment, we are unconscious of our own negative personality. Others, however, recognize it. Tensions disturbing fine body-balances interfere with sensitivity and responses. If we could see our own facial expressions objectively, reform would take place immediately.

INFANTILE BEHAVIOR OFTEN CARRIES OVER

Many small but persistent irritations beset our paths. If our unconscious habit, due to a pampered childhood, is to *demand* the "right of way," we may fail to recognize the equal importance of others at our side, and irritations result if we have to give them the preference. Temper arises, often to our real embarrassment.

We may dull our consciousness to the reports of our sensory organism by self-righteous moralizing over these matters, but to imagine that the sensations are not making their way through the nerve circuits habituated to receive them is false. We may be unconscious of them; nevertheless, they are contributing to the background of our inner environment.

In the confused issues between the conscious and the unconscious lie most of our difficulties. If we made a deeper study of what lies in the unconscious, and the amount of power it manifests in our daily behavior, we might come face to face with ourselves. This knowledge would evoke less ego, more self-respect. Upon our inner mechanisms depend the carrying out of our conscious demands.

If we have not known what to do with emotions in the past, the confusion still lingers in the memory pattern. Perhaps the criminal life of many a youth has been started by fragmentary, uncoordinated reactions never satisfactorily resolved in childhood. These break out when a new or current emotional situation becomes riotous. This condition may result from inherited tendencies which have had no intelligent guidance in childhood, but it is equally likely to have developed *around the ego* in childhood by *unwise distribution of praise and blame by elders.*

If we realize the universality of forces—that the moving stars belong to the same order of physical laws as ourselves, that the earth upon which we are standing is moving and changing and we with it—we will begin to feel ourselves minute and moving parts of the great whole.

In the presence of this concept of a constantly evolving universe and the feeling of the need for continual adjustment to it, the ego sinks into its proper place.

One aspect of the depth of the unconscious may be seen in the extreme depression, unexplainable even to oneself, which is often experienced when the unprepared ego meets the world. Group consciousness should be taught in the home. If this is not learned in early years willful stubbornness may cause many an emotional storm. To attempt without previous training to control negative reactions springing from the depths of the unconscious is like trying to calm a thunderstorm by a direct act of will.

Many chemical and physical forces mobilize for the thunderstorm. When all is ready an explosion takes place; both electric currents and water are precipitated earthward. However, a potential thunderstorm may be dissolved by changes taking place in the elements—shifting of wind currents both in speed and direction, changing of the condensation of moisture in the air, the effect of the sun upon the air—these and other movements and forces can change the conditions. But after the elements are all assembled for the storm, no prevention is possible.

The same is true of a strong emotional concentration in an individual. Many forces have assembled from both the past and present in preparation for a response. Only *movement* in the neuromuscular mechanism can effect a change in the chemical and physical balances. If the habit is inhibition without overt expression there is backfiring; if explosion, there is *temper expressed*. The first builds up inner conflict; the second tears down the confidence of others.

Both the thunderstorm and the human storm are assembled by environmental conditions changing chemical and physical balances. Learn to recognize them. In the human being these are pressures produced by the habit of unconsciously hiding, even from oneself, daily irritations and fatigue. One may be so habituated to the influence of small irritations that they are unrecognized, and hence no effort is made to dissolve them in action before their accumulated force is too great to be managed.

One may have a very high regard for his moral "self-control"; he may even feel superior to his fellows in this respect. This blinds him to the danger he is facing in these habitual inhibitions. He is self-deceived. The storm is mobilizing and must eventually explode in action. It will find outward expression or wreak vengeance upon his own organism—another form of explosion! Suppressed expression may lead to serious digestive disturbances and nervous breakdowns, as well as to continual discomforts.

To avoid all this difficulty one must increase his daily *awareness*, watch for the habits of petty irritation. When they rise to consciousness change the thinking; *make some movement which is agreeable and radiating*. If you feel like scowling, smile or whistle, at least iron out your face. Change of action will help to change the habit.

PHYSIOLOGICAL CONTROLS

New balances, chemical, physical, mechanical, are established by movement. Undesirable emotions may thus be dissolved, broken up. Rechemicalization takes place—a changed balance of forces!

For the marvelous behavior of our myriad bodily units there are *no outside controls* or hidden mystical sources of direction. The control lies within the structural composition and relationship of the organism; it lies in the grip of the inner man, conditioned by the outer man.

Much of our control is centered in the brain and spinal cord, admirably suited for this task; but these mechanisms, brain and spinal cord, are to be understood as composed of cellular units in precisely the same way as are other parts and systems of the human body. However, it is not the nervous system alone that manifests control. The destiny of growth placed in the chemical mysteries of the thyroid and pituitary glands, the fate of sugar transported to the liver, the sudden increase of muscular power when the adrenals start their dynamos are profound examples of physiological controls.

ACTIVATING HABITS

Ideas and ideals are activating habits no less than walking and breathing. Ask any person to reflect seriously upon that to which he has attached his faith; how he came to believe in it and just what there is about it that has so completely captured his imagination. Conflict exists immediately between logic and feeling. He will never dwell on *how* he came to believe it—he has long since forgotten that—but he will elaborate on *why* he believes as he does and it will be difficult indeed to turn these emotional reasons into logic. It seems heresy to doubt "facts" as he sees them. He has become habituated to his beliefs; he can rarely be moved from his stand. We react to emotions and think of reasons afterward. Emotions are not immediately changed by thinking because *thinking adjusts to the emotions.*

Our "vegetative systems" came first; our glands and nerves developed mechanisms as tools for the survival urge. The frontal brain developed as a tool for the emotions. Hence it is reasonable that our ideas and ideals are often activated more by feeling than by logic.

When emotional interferences have aborted the responses, thinking must be done to relieve the strain. Through it we arrive at "reasons" for our behavior. Comforting beliefs may be established and we rarely ask where they came from. Also disquieting beliefs may be established with just as illogical a background, but with more disastrous effects.

THE ROLE OF THE IMAGINATION

We do our building by the power of thought. Our creations take form according to our thoughts. But our imagination plays a large part in all thought activity. It vitalizes the picture for the use of the inner mechanisms. Through it our learning takes place.

We can never escape mental activity. It is with us night

and day. It has repercussions upon the entire organism. We can weep in sleep; we can laugh in sleep; we can talk and we can walk in sleep. The unconscious takes a very busy part in every hour of our twenty-four. In addition to the wisdom of the ages, the unconscious contains all the knowledge passed over to it through the imagination during the entire life of the individual. Our dreams offer us one proof of this fact.

In the first ten years the child has awakened to most of the realities of life and vitalized the mechanisms for meeting them. This is accomplished through the *imagination and identification.* This team forms the backbone of learning.

There is no better example of the power of the imagination than that evidenced in the baby learning to walk. Watch him. He has a faraway look in his eyes; he is looking inside, getting balance, trying to see himself doing as his elders are doing. Through identification with his elders he has tried many things with success. There is in the child an ever-increasing consciousness of outer movement and the effectiveness of it. He prepares for the event of walking by way of imagination and memories from within.

Baby's efforts in coordination can be aided only by giving him a sense of security and glory of accomplishment. With this encouragement, the memory patterns in the inner machinery combine for action; all preparations have been made and the great feat is a reality; he walks. Memories from the past and identification with the present are supported by the emotional *desire to do.* With the desire to do the responses are certain. The encouragement and applause of his elders strengthen his faith and surety. Thus he accomplishes.

UNCONSCIOUS REFLEXES AT WORK

The spine of a baby at birth is a string of movable bones with only one curve, a universal curve, throughout its length. Eventually this structure will develop four alternating curves which are necessary to make it secure as a weight-bearing column in an upright position.

For many weeks baby's back continues as one curve. His head hangs helplessly and must be carefully supported. But in the meantime baby is beginning to do a great many things—he cries more and laughs more, and his diaphragm and other respiratory muscles pull on the inside of his spine, to which they are attached. He doubles up his knees and kicks more and more vigorously. He clenches his fists and grasps at things. And all of these motions are producing two new curves in his spine. In his unconscious he is preparing his structure for the upright position. When the muscles attached to the freer parts of the spinal column at the waist and the neck have gained enough strength, baby has developed alternate curves in his spine. He can then carry his weight upright. He can hold up his head and he can sit up. His spine is balanced. Bones and muscles cooperate to keep it so.

When the organism has been properly prepared by exercise and structural growth, functional response appears. A healthy normal baby, as he learns to sit, stand, and finally walk, gains his balance by many daily muscular motions, all leading toward the great accomplishments—standing and walking.

The desire to stand and walk should be left to the child's initiative. Children vary greatly in their desire to accomplish walking. This should never be forced, as the spinal curves are being prepared to support their assembled loads in the upright position through muscular development of the base and the opposing curves. By kicking, creeping, grasping, by head movements and bone growth, the spinal column prepares itself for the task assigned to it by nature, that is, to support and move a mobile structure. This accomplished, baby becomes conscious of his power to engage in expanded activities.

BIOLOGICAL PATTERNS IN THE UNCONSCIOUS

The apparatus for locomotion and for breathing appeared simultaneously in the racial pattern. They are intimately related through mechanical and nervous tie-ups, and together they are related very closely to the heart and the circulatory system.

The parts of a man's skeletal and muscular systems which operate to maintain the spinal curves and keep the trunk erect are very closely related to the bony and muscular parts involved in breathing. The mechanisms for breathing are intimately tied to both the visceral organs and the skeletal muscles. Control of oxygen supply and balance of stance are important functions of survival. This fact protects the organism in such extreme activities as fighting, running, or "holding the stance."

The course of development involved in the erect carriage is reflected in the history of the individual. In the embryo, arms and legs develop rather late, but arms and hands are more fully developed functionally at birth than legs. The legs and the pelvis do not begin to get their later proportions until they are needed for walking. The creeping stage prepares for the dramatic event of walking.

THE RESERVES OF THE UNCONSCIOUS

The attitude of the well and active person is so animated by purpose that it excites little comment. Skilled sportsmen, in whom unity of the body systems is evident and motions outrun thoughts, are usually radiantly healthy. The whole picture of bright hair, fresh skin, clear eyes, and elasticity accompany bodily unity, a prolongation of youth.

In contrast to this picture of youthful perfection is the picture of decadence, the letting go as a result of illness, of depression, of age, or of accident. But triumphing over this darker side of life, the flame of the spirit may still project a powerful urge toward the upholding of one part by another. The blind, the lame, the deformed, the deaf, when thrown off balance often find special forces to compensate in some manner for their infirmities.

Blind Milton, Clemenceau at his strongest in ripened years, crippled Snowden, former Chief of the British Exchequer, Sarah Bernhardt, the two Roosevelts—the list is long, indicating that where the physical body is handicapped, all forces of the being rise to compete for first place in furtherance of the purposes of the individual. Such a rare and special triumph shows the spiritual ability of life to make adjustments.

DAILY-HABIT FORMING

Form daily habits of changing patterns of behavior consciously from irritable action or inhibitory tension to some positive expression. This will affect future reactions when emergencies arise. When the change in directions and velocities of your own forces and those of your outer environment make quick reactions necessary, your daily habits already established in the unconscious will speedily determine your behavior in meeting the larger issues. All future reactions lie in the habits of your daily thinking and doing.

Your responses in small matters day by day will set the pattern by which you will act when the direction and velocities of your own forces are increased. A new habit must be integrated in the thinking and the doing if you are not to be surprised into unwelcome speech and action. Emotional satisfactions will eventually follow. Upon them will depend to a large extent your future reactions.

Speedy adjustment to disturbances from within, as well as to environmental changes, requires incessant adaptation. It affects the mental and emotional processes of the human being as well as his physical balance. Apply corrective methods quickly in all small matters of maladjustments daily.

CHAPTER XVI

The Language of the Body

People sit and stand as they live. Ideas behind the leg, arm, and head arrangements speak through the body parts. The explorer and the pioneer stand straight, the prisoner and the slave crouch, the saint leans forward, the overseer and the magnate lean back. Soldiers and ministers have the distinctive attitudes of men who hold doctrines, those deepest in the doctrines displaying the greatest rigidity. A policeman has the coordination that gets eye, hand, and holster instantly together and the strong flexible feet that indicate he can run. The stuff of the ages goes into man's thinking, is interpreted, and comes out through the body again. Personality goes into structure—by denial or affirmation, into person again. The thinking body evolves. It is an aspect of life evolution.

There is, then, a language of the body that denotes function and personality. It speaks before the tongue speaks and may even oppose words, rapidly saying one thing with the body while speech says another. Emerson expressed this truth when he wrote, "What you are thunders so—I cannot hear what you say."

The body has a pattern for listening while the ear listens,

and for seeing while the eye sees. It can rapidly assume patterns of fear, boasting, sickness, courage. These moods are patterns of movement and the movement responses to emotional thinking. Thus through the imagination behavior is the presentation of meaning—life's *purposes* mold living substance.

THE HUMAN RECEIVING AND SENDING SET

As you, an organism, sit reading this page, you are aware of your world by an intricate and extended series of nerves, called *receptors* by the physiologists. They are the endings of the sensory nerves—nerves of sensation. Those on the outside, acquainting you with your surroundings, are called the "external receptors." But there are also those within the body, bringing you awareness of comforts and discomforts of the inner man. They receive information regarding the condition of the blood, the flow of digestive juices, and the action of all organs of the body. These are called "internal receptors." Their reports rarely rise into consciousness unless some part of your organic self requires attention. But often, if you are engaged in intensely interesting mental pursuit, they may have difficulty pushing through for their pressing need. However, at times the receiving mechanism spills over, as it were, and we become aware of a pain in the back, palpitation of the heart, or a sinking feeling in the pit of the stomach.

Under ordinary conditions these internal stimuli may in general make for a comfortable sense of well-being. When something is wrong, however, it is the better part of wisdom to "listen" before it is too late. In a state of fatigue, for example, we could often save ourselves much trouble and poisonous congestion if we listened to the "wisdom of the body" (Dr. Walter Cannon's term for inherent intelligence) before becoming overfatigued. Exhaustion makes a simple remedy difficult. Frequently the muscles of the inner organism, as well as those of the outer, are crying for oxygen and water. Sometimes supplying these needs alone will take care of the difficulty, but quite often *complete rest* is the only solution. Short periods of rest taken often when doing concentrated work, either physical or mental, are very helpful.

The internal receiving-mechanism carries a vast amount of information to the nerve centers, but this mechanism is automatic in its behavior. Impulses from the internal receptors incessantly pour their reports into headquarters. One may care nothing about the hydrogen-ion concentration of the blood (the scientist's words to describe the amount of acid units present in the blood stream), but a group of cells in the brain stem, known as the "respiratory center," *must* pay attention to this ion content, for they regulate the breathing of the organism in response to its needs. Whenever the acid concentration in the blood changes, the nerves of the breathing apparatus are stimulated, and breathing muscles automatically respond.

To the novice, the flow of impulses from the alimentary canal reporting on the state of the digestive tract exit only in fact—or in consciousness—when reports are unfavorable. But to the diagnostician, they are a continuous series of indispensable value in determining the state of the living organism.

The external receiving-mechanisms give us information concerning the external environment, and as the information arrives in the spinal cord and brain we become aware of what is taking place around us. The external receptors extend over the entire surface of the body and in numerous places are elaborated into exceedingly complex structures, such as in the eye, the ear, and the nerves of heat and cold in the skin. The latter special nerves in the skin can easily be tested by dropping the lead end of a pencil repeatedly upon the back of the hand; some spots will feel cold, others will feel warm, at the point of the lead.

OUR MODIFIERS

Added to these channels of information, there are inherited predispositions, urges, and drives that modify the activity of the receptors and favor the actions of an individual along certain lines.

There is no way in which one may receive information,

guidance, inspiration, pleasure or pain except through the operation of instinct and the activities of the receptor mechanism. If, for example, the eye receptor is destroyed, the organism cannot receive light waves and hence is blind. If the ear receptor is lost, hearing vanishes and sound waves beat upon the organism impatient to impart these messages.

One may close the eyelids, excluding light, and vision for that moment ceases; one may taste only bitter and so avoid sweets. But so long as the organism remains in contact with any aspect of the environment, that aspect beats ceaselessly upon it. Man is then a receiving mechanism. The convenient term *you* or *I* has nothing to do with the reception. All of us receive like messages but each correlates and responds to them in his own particular way. When we are well, the very unobtrusiveness of our bodily workings favors our ignorance and failure to appreciate them.

THE TOTAL SITUATION

This receiving, correlating, responding mechanism called man receives through the sensory nervous system, correlates through the brain and nerve cells, and responds through motor nerves, muscles, organs, and glands. So close is this relationship of the external and internal environment to the organism that science has coined a phrase to describe the fact: "the total situation." Thus the organism does not exist in a vacuum, nor can one think of an individual apart from the environment, both external and internal, that encompasses him. We cannot escape this night or day.

Think of a friend you know well, a passing stranger you know not at all, or a striking character in history. Why do you know your friend and not the passing stranger? Because of the many external environmental situations that your friend brings to your memory, and his responses, so characteristic of his internal environment, that make him what he is. And the stranger? Him you know only with respect to his clothes, the tilt of his hat, the street he walks upon, the house he enters, the dog that barks at him and what he does when it barks. Only the trained, astute observer could read in his walk or his facial expression the story of his internal strains.

Man's whole integration with his world is a matter of skin, nerves, bones, muscles, blood, brain, and glands, an army of working cells. He is being molded from outside and churning inside as he becomes a personality. He differs from his fellows in individual correlation only.

CORRELATION

Coming into the organism at any one moment may be the sound of rushing waters, the call of birds, the grayness of the day, sounds of merriment from the tennis court, the thought of the study within, with desk piled high and beckoning to work. If the organism could live in a vacuum for thirty years and then suddenly be catapulted into such a maelstrom of sensations it would be as helpless as a newborn babe.

In the matured organism, however, these inrushing messages may be correlated exactly to highly variable ends. But there is no machine-made response, no set routine, no irresistible outcome. Choices must be made. There are habits, of course, but beyond these there are a thousand possible paths to be followed. Anticipations arrive to influence our choices. There comes the urge to smoke as a whiff of a good cigar comes floating through the open window, so one smokes.

Here they come—all the messages from a far-flung receptor system now brought to a focus, perhaps one favorite selected for elaboration and further pursuit. One chooses to work, play, or smoke. These are the superficial signs of *correlation*. The deeper ones, however, are not so easily discernible.

MECHANISMS AND FORCES

Life, we find, is a ceaseless activity of energy as seen in an objective universe. In all structures, animate or inanimate, energy is evident and forces are active. Through close observation we may detect the kind ot energy acting and the kind of response in the substances through which it acts.

In all organized motion there is an applied force operating on the separate units of weight of the structure. In one machine the force may be electricity; in another, steam; in another, expanding gas. In the human body it is nervous energy generated within.

Our living force more closely resembles electricity in its behavior than any other form of energy. Minute impulses travel speedily over "wires" designated to carry them. Catch their messages in the alerted stage. Attention must be arrested or reconditioning will be difficult.

Watch an elk in one of our natural parks as he grazes on a hillside. Silence is everywhere. Now a twig snaps and instantly the animal raises its head, pointing it toward the direction of the noise, ears cocked forward, eyes focusing, nostrils straining for the scent, every receptor on the alert to receive further information.

The physiologists would describe the flow of blood toward the head end of the alerted animal. They would portray the increased activity of the brain and spinal cord, the increased heartbeat, the tensing of the muscles, and the reports of the receptors, both internal and external. They would point out that the powerful chemical adrenalin is being poured from the adrenal glands into the blood stream. All these preparations are made that the responses may be adequate for a life-saving situation. Preparations for running or fighting as need demands!

PREPARATIONS FOR RESPONSE

Correlation is a *mental* and *physiological* process. Receiving and correlating take up at least two thirds of the complete experience in time and space. We call this preparation. The one-third time remaining is absorbed in the response. Time, as we conceive it, is no factor in these activities. Response is automatically accelerated or retarded according to the need. Note the individual difference in the time factor of human responses in escaping the dangers of everyday life. There is no *consciousness* of the time element. For example, consider our response to the streetcar that barely missed us or to the automobile making an unexpected left turn. These present to each of us an instantaneous need for an accurate time-space calculation. The response depends upon the alertness of our receptors and their coordinating centers. What is the sudden decision by the somnambulist to rise and walk in sleep when dreaming of escape from fire or flood but the following of an established pathway of unconscious effort? He rarely suffers bodily injury in this act.

We have all seen in cat or dog, in cow or horse, and in man himself, this preparation for danger and escape. What we do not see is the remarkable series of transformations within the organism, the adaptations, the circulatory alterations, the muscular contractions, the glandular secretions that stand in intimate relation to the varying changes which run throughout the alert organism. In short, the organism receives myriad messages and then, on the basis of its *past experiences,* proceeds to *organize itself* in relation to them. This is preparation—deep and purposive. The response is automatic.

WISDOM OF NATURE

In your reactions to varying situations you have built for yourself a body of knowledge. The memories composing this structure are not located in one particular place or organ, but fill every cell of your entire being, in a pattern accumulated through past experience. Habits are thus built up and their controlling influence affects your every act.

Knowledge by itself will function in an emergency only in so far as habits of quick observation, consciously or unconsciously, reveal elements in the emergency identical with some which have been experienced previously.

The correlation of these received messages is in part learned and in part the product of nature. The vast array of adjustments that marshal themselves through the internal mechanism marches forth in each individual determining his actions. Nature, that wise conservator of life, knows *how* to produce adrenalin in a moment of danger, *how* to uncover latent energies in muscles, *how* to release protective mechanisms in eye, in heart, and in the hearing and balancing apparatus.

THE UNION OF INSTINCT AND LEARNING

The individual is constructed to receive information regarding the state of his internal cellular being and the external world of his physical environment.

At a very early age a child must learn to adjust to his immediate environment, to people and to things, to meet shocks of various kinds, emotional, mental and physical. Like the birth shock, weaning is also a shock to a child and requires real intelligence by the mother to guide him safely through. The art of cleanliness, a safe steering through the awakening curiosity of primitive functions, the unhappiness with hunger, the fear of loud noises and of falling and the rage at the restriction of movement, all present real problems which the wise parent tries to solve.

Difficulty from any of these shocks may, if not patiently handled, present serious inhibitions later. Baby is busy building his new memory-charts, and patience, wisdom, and understanding by his elders is needed or repercussions may occur later in life. An extreme example is the following: The most disagreeable nurse of his babyhood surrounded this boy with pink—drapes, bedding, and nurse's uniform—and afterward, when all this was apparently forgotten, whenever his wife appeared in a pink gown he became actively ill. It took some time and the attention of a psychiatrist to uncover the facts.

LIFE IS A CONTINUED RESPONSIVENESS

Ceaselessly, upon the cellular organism of man, beats the world of his internal and external environments. Reception provokes response and correlation guides it. What we get from the world determines in part what we give. But those deterministic

qualities of sex cells which produce us and give us our inheritance also influence the response. Regardless, however, of
qualities and quantities, there is response so long as the organism remains alive. The impulse comes over the receptor system,
is correlated with respect to learning, habits, strength, weak-
nesses, instinctive patterns, and then, like a stick of dynamite,
instantly activated by its inserted cap, comes the response!

That spark called "life" distinguishes protoplasm from other
active substances. It gives to the protozoans—the single-celled
creatures, amoeba, stentor, paramecium—the same possibility to
react to the physical environment enjoyed by the higher animals.
Life, continued responsiveness, continued evolution from one
form to another, from a lower plane to a higher plane!

THE INSTINCTIVE

Many of man's reactions are instinctive at their root, like
the fear of falling and of loud noises. Most fears undoubtedly
are trained rather then instinctive. The force called instinct, so
highly developed in animals, almost seems intelligence at times.
When we see instinct in dogs developed to a high degree we
sometimes prefer to interpret it as intelligence, but we know
that dogs cannot analyze their behavior as men can.

Also in man we often feel that intelligence manifests a
high degree of the instinctive. But would man instinctively walk
upright or talk sense or nonsense, if he were born in an environment where these reactions could never be observed? Probably
not. Observe the account of the "Indian Wolf Children," as
reported by Sir William Fuller in his *Science of Ourselves*. The
wolves in India, who carry off many children, do not kill them
all. In 1849 Major General William Sleeman gave the first au-
thentic report of those children after having seen several rescued
from the wolves. These children ran on all fours, had no articulate
speech, and preferred to run with dogs instead of men. One of
these adult children, found sitting with a wolf at the entrance
to a burrow, was captured and placed in a missionary asylum
in 1867. In the following twenty-eight years he never attained

the erect position, never learned to speak. The only marked change of behavior was his eating with his fingers instead of burying his nose in the dish, wolf-fashion. When digression is too great, as in this example, reconditioning is difficult unless the inner velocities are stimulated by a keen *desire to do*. It is through identification of the baby with its elders that direction of the inherited patterns for movement are determined in time and space.

OUR IGNORANCE OF SELF

Many of the most commonplace responses in man still remain unanalyzed and very largely unappreciated. Examples of this are seen in such so-called "natural functions" as walking, breathing, coughing, sneezing, sleeping, laughing, and many similar, everyday experiences which we all enjoy without questioning their subtle technique.

The simple act of eating is really quite a complicated thing if analyzed from the standpoint of mechanical technique and organic functioning. At mealtime one sits down to a pleasantly appointed table. There is appetite. There is food. The cells engaged in producing digestive juices are informed by messages from the receptors of sight and smell and at once respond.

Chemical preparations are made by the internal mechanisms of digestion. Soon the inner mechanisms dealing with time-space movement must take over. The tongue is one of the dextrous members of this organization. It must shift different types, weights, and sizes of material with speed and accuracy from the "cutters" to "grinders" in order to deal with the food we are enjoying. And we may carry on a conversation at the same time with our neighbor!

Man the egotist may well pause to take account of stock, to find where in his ignorance he is interfering with such a well-balanced, effective mechanism. In urging more sensory education, more emphasis on sound, color, form, movement, and more attention to *habitual emotional life*, we are not pleading for less intellect but for *better use* of the intellect in recognizing and understanding what has been and is being received.

Much depends on the capacity of dynamic man to increase his sensitivity in receiving, to speed and perfect his correlations, and to strengthen his power of response. Growth, expansion of personality in constructive living, is thus incorporated in the language of his body.

An organism so receiving, so correlating, and so responding continually integrates the spirit to conquer, not other men, but the forces that are bearing upon him from within and without. He daily reassembles his God-given powers to meet them. "He who conquereth himself is greater than he who taketh a walled city."

CHAPTER XVII

The Ego in Behavior

In the process of civilization, the ego has become more and more emphasized. Individuals have aspired toward self-glorification and aggrandizement. Rostand's play, *Chanticleer*, illustrates to what degree of importance we can elevate ourselves when we insist upon our own particular form of egotism. Chanticleer never dreamed of vaster horizons than his own barnyard, and proclaimed himself a mouthpiece for the cry of the earth to the sky. "My song springs forth so clear that the horizon obeys," he cries triumphantly and, suiting the attitude of his body to his feelings, stiffening up his cock's comb and puffing out his chest, he struts about as a lord in his little community.

Ego is a small word. But it holds all the potentialities of individual inflation and deflation, and the dire disasters accompanying these two extremes. It is built upon emotion and it thrives upon emotional satisfactions. When these are lacking the world is an empty place indeed and the individual suffers a depression and confusion which he is unable to understand.

EGO, A PART OF THE WHOLE

If we think of the play and balance of the unseen forces in the human organism, the ego tends to lose itself in the unity

of the whole. Life understood in terms of coordinated velocities of cellular activity brings a deep realization of the essence
of our living forces. This view of the organism immeasurably
broadens life. The imposition of a wilful "I" that attempts to
force a change of behavior upon the age-old unconscious is
futile. We only block habitual patterns of behavior, which form
the background of all present behavior.

There are no divisions in living protoplasm, no classifica-
tions in nature, nothing but the unity of the organism in nature's
larger *whole*. No room for an aggrandized ego here! To achieve
a synthesis, to put the ego in its place, we must understand our
biological nature and must also recognize the play of the various
social forces that reach their tenuous fingers from a long and
lingering past to shape and mold the present.

When we realize that others are being played upon and
conditioned by the same set of forces as ourselves, we can have
respect for our own ego as well as that of others, giving neither
undue importance.

INDIVIDUAL BEHAVIOR

My behavior is important to me, your behavior is important
to you, and that of both of us is important to our fellow beings.
The question is, does my behavior, does your behavior, demand
a "special place in the sun"? Is the ego assuming undue importance?

We have alternate moments of irritation and melancholy
to disturb our peace of mind and our relation with our fellows,
but as thinking men and women each of us has an acute sense
of responsibility for his own behavior. To be successful in the
understanding and interpretation of our own behavior and that
of others, we must realize that most of their behavior *is in the
same category as our own*. All behavior stems from sensory
reports. Correlation is the only individual problem.

We have a tendency to explain our own behavior to ourselves in terms of outside causes. We behaved thus and so because people or things did this or that. There are many hidden
causes from both within and without underlying every situation,
and more often than not the cause selected is not the true cause

at all, or at best only one of many. It may be very remote from the original causes, so we may be led far astray in the confusion of self-justification and the quest for an "alibi"—both unconscious attempts to save the ego. We may thus build up so-called "mechanisms of escape or defense" of which we would never dream in our saner moments. In this mental fog and emotional confusion lie many causes of behavior, rational and irrational, which cannot be analyzed by consciously moralizing over them. There are assembled many unseen causes laid deep in the memory patterns of our forgotten yesterdays.

When energy is wasted mentally, emotionally, or physically, it reacts upon all the systems of the human being. Futile thought over hypothetical problems that may never arise affects the nervous system and the bodily processes. Uncontrolled emotion in the midst of mental and physical effort reacts in the same way. Faulty bodily adjustment, creating an unnecessary expenditure of energy in maintaining balance of individual parts, has equally far-reaching and evil effects.

We know that balance is the key to the conservation and economic use of energy in the behavior of *any* structure. There is continuous adjustment and readjustment between the environment and the individual. That is what living means—a constant interplay among our ancient animal mechanism, our historical inheritance, and our present feeling and thinking. We are usually unconscious of these processes, but they are combined in responsibility for our actions.

Our story-writers are able to exhibit plausibly the reflections and emotions of human beings. We make an unconscious muscular response to moods of every kind as we read about our fellows or meditate upon their words and actions. Forces—biological, chemical and mechanical, social and spiritual—interplaying and acting one upon the other, have been the determinants of human behavior throughout the ages.

CONTROL VERSUS COMMAND

Irrespective of our gifts and powers it ill behooves any of us to pride himself upon his control of self or of others. We are controlled far more than we are at once able or even willing to recognize. One reason for our lack of recognition of this truth is the fact that "strengthening the will" has been in the past a favorite theme of those who would guide others to success and efficiency.

"Moral duty" has been expressed in "will power," and bodily habits of inhibitions and tensions have followed in the trail of this training. Behavior patterns are physiological, and morals belong to the social order, not to the physiological. "The greatest good to the greatest number" is a worthy ambition, but we must find a way of disciplining ourselves which will utilize our active patterns of behavior instead of producing more tensions.

Commanding our rampant natural inclinations makes us civilized persons. Directing them into useful channels of behavior is the best form of discipline. Inhibition is well-cloaked in "will power." "Will power" as applied in the past is "setting the heel" upon driving human forces. The stronger the pressure, the greater the "willful" effort to control; strains and tensions and inhibitions result. Willfulness in one is met by willfulness in another. This habit grows; resistance stimulates resistance. Momentary explosions which we observe in the behavior of ourselves and our many friends are the result of the accumulation of these forced inhibitions and strains. When the strain is too great we "spill over."

If high steam-pressure is developed in a hermetically sealed boiler, one must prepare for results—an explosion is the inevitable outcome. The same is true of the human being when more pressure develops than the individual can endure. As in the steam boiler, it must find vent. Energy confined within must eventually burst out. We explode!

Inhibitions in themselves are never valuable to an active organism habituated through eons of time to respond in a purposeful way as the need arises. To the well-informed the "will," the *moral whip of past generations*, is found to be fixity in a finely balanced mechanism, blocking the open pathways for neuromuscular response. We must find a type of self-discipline which goes with nature's constructive pattern of behavior. *Self-*

determinations are valuable if they are intelligently guided into constructive action.

The individual who prides himself upon his "will power" is holding on to static patterns of moral duty. In the light of present knowledge, "will power" is found to be muscular tension which aborts the purposes of active expression. Confusions arise.

TEMPER AND WILLFULNESS

Habitually buried tensions develop into illogical, irritable responses to apparently unimportant events and situations. These reactions are often ascribed by ourselves and others to "hypersensitiveness." We take too many of these unanalyzed behavior patterns for granted, and attribute them to the "temperament" of our friends and of ourselves. Why not do an intelligent job of *analysis?* In an effort to find a solution for these irritable responses we must recognize that *daily habits* create the pattern for all future behavior in relation to the trying situations of life.

A simple word spoken by a close friend or by a member of our family may *seem* to be the *cause* lighting the fuse for explosion, but there are as many causes back of the habits of "willfulness" or *inhibited temper* as there are inherited patterns of behavior. Temper exploded is often more harmful to the person exploding than to the accused aggressor. It is rarely understood by the accused, and often deeply regretted by the accuser. The accuser does not understand the tensions accumulated by his daily irritations, which terminated in the explosion.

Many an individual has wasted prayer over his explosive temper. This is of no avail unless he uses some intelligent effort to correct it. Inhibited temper builds up deep tensions. When the limit of endurance has been reached, an explosion is inevitable; neither magic nor momentary prayer can prevent it if *artificial, super-imposed control*, with its daily inhibitions, has been the practice. *Pride of endurance* and self-righteousness is never an indulgence of the integrated personality. Determination to recognize and to meet the daily small irritations with effective action is the positive way to change these habits to more intelligent ones. *Endure less, act more.* Action may be guided into helpful channels. Prideful endurance can never be. Daily patience in small things, with a constructive response to them, leads to greater integration.

The discipline of *self-analysis* might encourage more brotherly love and more patience with ourselves and others. Impatience with oneself is as destructive as is impatience with others. We should make constructive efforts toward correction of these *negative daily habits.*

The difficulty in our effort to change these thinking habits is the *fixity of the idea* that the *cause* of our irritation lies outside ourselves. However, if we analyze more closely, we find that we ignored today the very thing which caused us to explode yesterday. There are other causes than those which appear on the surface setting up conditions within ourselves for irritable behavior—uninteresting work, indigestion, headache, disturbing office-problems, lack of chemical balance. All these produce deep tensions. We feel these discomforts, but place them on a moral basis and establish endurance—"self-control"—with pride in our behavior. It would be more intelligent to find some type of action helpful to the situation. Changing the thinking will change the conditions. Do something, and *find satisfaction in the doing. Cease the struggle to inhibit and to endure.* Give the imagination play, and dramatize facts valuable to the situation.

Much of the value in the various cults, and in fact in religion itself, is due to a type of devotion to a particular philosophy of life which enables one to dramatize with satisfaction his self-discipline. But what are the real issues of life? We must know the facts relating to them. *Facts* may be dramatized as well as fiction. The constructive use of the imagination binds the thinking and the emotions together. On the other hand, if one presumes to present to another bare facts which conflict with emotional beliefs and conventional practices, he is very likely to draw a curtain between himself and his listener at just those points where the stated facts pierce the old superstitions, the pet prejudices, and the ever-present fears. These still unconsciously control his thinking.

What relation have mental and emotional processes to muscular strains? The muscular concomitant of so-called "temptation" has, so far as we know, never been carefully investigated. *Fighting* for God and Country, *defending* the right, attacking evil, and putting the devil to rout, all suggest muscular activity. Wholehearted action offers no physical harm. Engaging in a single enterprise is ever exhilarating. There is no muscular backfire. But the very word "temptation" implies moral *struggles*, *resisting* the seductions of the devil, suggests an *urge to do* the thing we are trying not to do. So, in addition to all other strains, there are moral, muscular tensions quite as real as fighting off an aggressive, mad dog or, as in former days, holding tight to a runaway horse.

What association have doubt, anxiety, and worry with muscular strain? One suffering from these afflictions often says, "I feel under such a strain," or, "I am so tense," or, "I am all tied up." And why not? Every movement is the result of contracting muscles. To be in doubt is not to know what to do. There are double sets of muscles, which act in opposite ways. One set extends the hand, another retracts it. We are offered a cocktail and may, if we are so disposed, tend to extend our hand, but the thought that we are on the point of violating a pledge, or setting a bad example, will bring the opposing set of muscles into action. As we hesitate in a state of indecision we are using both sets. Does the sense of indecision produce the strain, or the strain the disagreeable feeling of doubt? If we lightly accept or refuse the drink we find no tension, and probably the muscles undergo little perceptible change. If we feel a sense of apprehension an unmistakable tension of facial muscles is often evident.

Fear and anger are agencies of defense. They are valuable assets if we have respect for them and learn their proper guidance. They are factors in the behavior of everyone. We shall never understand them by trying to control them. A saner *use* of them is what we must learn.

Fear analyzed is found to be the first step toward anger. The alerted animal must experience fear before anger can prepare the mechanisms for defense. There can be no bravery without fear. In man fear utilized produces caution, a valuable asset in civilization. So accept fear and anger shamelessly and learn to deal with them.

Only brave men confess to having fear. They have proven their bravery in the face of danger and they have no need to build the ego. Ego deflation has no terrors for them. Their habits of behavior are constructive, active, positive. They have found their integration in life.

If the forces of anger are turned into the defense of an ideal, instead of the defense of an ego, they too have great value. In either case the *old switches open up,* call into play the adrenals, heart, and thyroid, and inhibit the digestive and procreative functions. Then the working mechanism is ready for defense or flight and is raised to the levels of great activity. In modern man, when no bodily response is made, muscles which have been prepared for action are tense and uncomfortable, inhibition replacing expansive movement.

When, in a fear situation, the animal "froze" to escape detection, he was very active indeed. While his muscles held his framework he still had his decisions to make about escape or flight. If "to fight" was the decision, the mechanisms of *anger* must take over. They must raise the chemical activity to increase the energy in the muscles of response. Coordination for eye focus, teamwork of the extremities, weight control, and breathing acceleration are essentials for survival. Rage is the tool activating this organization of forces.

In man likewise, the urge to express matches the stimulation. It either turns out or it turns in. Inhibition, movement turning in, produces muscular tensions. Poisonous ash from the fires of combustion accumulate, and in time affect even the organic smooth muscles. Inhibition is a type of response to stimulation, and can be just as habit-forming as positive fulfillment of impulses for expansive movement.

HABITUAL FEAR-ADJUSTMENTS

Two people witnessing an automobile accident may react quite differently to it. One leaps to the rescue. The one in whom the inhibition of fear has become a daily habit may faint and drop to the ground. Organic muscles as well as structural muscles have gripped the individual, interfering with the supply of blood to his brain.

Both persons received the same original impression. Both witnessed the catastrophe. In one, emotional appreciation carried through to effective rhythms of response. Mechanical and physiological preparations found expression and power through the unconscious. The habit of the positive organism carried no inhibitions to the conscious. This person's energies were released on demand.

A similar type of response may be seen in the courageous individual after a great personal defeat. The personality begins to come back with force. He first acts with the pose of endurance, continues with the forced smile, and may even go on through satire. The expression of bitterness is the catharsis through which he returns to normal. Our basis for judgment should be whether he shows us the psychology and physiology of the struggle immoderately, or just enough. What direction does he give to life? Has he a solution?

Temper is the greatest blessing and the greatest curse of man. Temper is the outcome of fear. Without it the animal or man would never have survived. Fear is the stimulus that alerts the animal for action. Anger must follow very closely if he ever has the courage to face his enemy.

Fear always raises the center of gravity in the alerted body, sharpens the wits, increases the sensory activity. The state of alertness is taking account of possibilities of encroachment upon individual rights. In the animal this meant quickly appraising elements of danger to self or offspring. Anger must follow fear to prepare the deep bodily mechanisms for escape or fight. Hormones must be poured into the blood to increase muscular power. All forces of the living engines, muscles, must be amplified. The fires of living must be kept high and oxygen supply free for increased use. Living energy is burning the fuels of life rapidly. Anger is the mechanism which keeps this supply coming. Fear and anger are so intermingled in the habits of the living mechanism that their understanding and guidance are of utmost importance to modern man. He still struggles for survival.

The scientific-research laboratories have given us many facts about fear and anger which we should incorporate into our everyday thinking. The devoted investigators in this field, Doctors Cannon, Pavlov, and Crile, to mention but a few, have demonstrated the effect of fear and anger on organic life. Their findings indicate conclusively that the tensions produced by aborted movement, inhibited because of fear and anger, lie back of many organic disturbances, even of the most serious nature.

Accept fear and anger as a part of your survival equipment. Divorce them from the moral aspects and find a way to guide their expression. Neither run away from the recognition of them nor let them run away with you. You can learn to command action in relation to them and to guide them into constructive channels of behavior.

Choices may be made. One is responsible only for action, *not for feeling.* As there can be no direct dealing with the emotion itself, new thought-habits only can be encouraged and through them a better integration and response attained. Dissipate fear and anger by action; *it cannot be done by inhibition.*

Utilize the stimulated energies in some form of movement and find satisfaction in the doing.

INNER CONFLICTS

Hunger, sex, fear, and anger have been analyzed as survival behavior only since an organized society made it necessary for the individual to choose a type of behavior in relation to his primary instincts that would benefit and not injure the greatest majority. An organized society provides punishment for the selfish member who ignores this necessity. But inhibited action—action turned in—produces conflicts, and conflicts also are destructive, and produce destructive behavior.

Every thought changes bodily action. If there is conflict between the concept or ideal and the instinctive response, something must give way. We may be unaware of many such conflicts. Often the fear of failure, for example, will not show itself openly even to its victim. That depends upon habits already established. If he has been brought up to feel that fear is not indulged in by decent or courageous persons, his fear may manifest itself in digestive disturbances, heart palpitation, dry mouth, chills, or sweats. Through the sympathetic nervous system these organic disturbances will act upon his consciousness from deep within quite automatically to convince the sufferer that he is really ill. He unconsciously arrives at an escape or a protective behavior and fear has conquered. The fearful person never quite faces himself. Face facts and highlight them in the imagination.

When considering our "army of workers" (our cells), even the "I" passes out of the picture and becomes only a term of convenience. The complaint of the coward, "I am afraid," does not imply an inner being distinct from the organism that feels timid and afraid. The words, "I am afraid," are the result of a series of previous experiences when the receptors brought in certain messages to which confused responses were made with no satisfactory results. They make us feel unprotected—exposed to alien elements.

A child encounters a stray animal on a dark road, and messages come over his receptors, followed by response of his whole organism. He finds himself running; he has a rapidly beating heart, adrenalin pours into the blood, breathing is accelerated, and many cellular responses are being made which are labeled *fear*, and of which he may or may not be conscious as separate experiences.

The simple fact remains—the individual always responds to the messages received over the receptor system, and the whole organism reacts in its characteristic way, whether this is desired or not. In the case of fear and the effort to escape a real or imagined danger, running might be controlled, but not glandular, heart, and breathing acceleration. Overt action can be controlled, but the *emotional drive* lies beyond conscious command. The emotion is a group of sensations coordinated in the unconscious.

Timidity is often expressed in unreasonable panics over perfectly harmless situations. For example consider the fear in elevator or train travel, crowded theaters, or large social functions—harmless, but to the sufferer, dreaded occasions. He may have been conditioned in childhood to fight or resist "insignificant" daily emotions, which some form of directed action could have corrected. The person so afflicted may prove courageous under more difficult or dangerous situations.

The effect of fighting an emotion is to increase it. Hiding it is another way of fighting it. *Both methods harbor it.* The person who fights his fears usually considers himself a supersensitive person and is, deep down, rather proud of it.

We may be pretty sure that anger is also tied in with these fear reactions—anger that the demands of the ego are ignored by some individual or even by life itself. This anger may have been so deeply buried that the only expression of it is self-pity. Self-pity is like strong drink—there is considerable kick in its negative reactions. "Expression" or "repression" produces the resultant headache in oneself or in somebody else. If self-virtuous, the headache stays at home.

The immediate stoppage of the digestive organs due to

arousing fear, anxiety, or anger is now a proven fact. The terrified cat at the top of the elm, his muscular strength greatly enhanced by his adrenalin secretion, stops digestion because of his more pressing needs. Rescue him and he curls up in his corner and is soon fast asleep, recovering his equilibrium. His chemical and mechanical balances quickly readjust.

Man, however, being the only animal that can be *afraid all the time,* prolongs his conflicts even after the danger is past, through memory of past fears and anticipation of future ones. Proust died of introspection long before he died of pneumonia, burned out by the chemistry of the many volumes of *Remembrance of Things Past.*

Life is either a harmonious adjustment between emotions or a constant struggle between emotions. Emotional pressure must be met often. If we could work off through bodily expression all emotional drives, as the uninhibited animal does, fixed tensions would not result. But fortunately social amenities are with us to stay; man must grapple with his tensions as best he may—the more intelligently, the better.

Fixed tensions are the "static" contraction of *muscles gripping bones*—muscles crying for the privilege to perform their function—to *move bones.* Fixed tensions will turn in and destroy one with a final explosion, or they will break their bonds and spend their fury upon someone else. Capping Vesuvius benefits no one!

INHERITED MECHANISMS

In prehistoric days man was faced with the constant need of decision to fight or to run. If danger threatened, he lifted his head to the position of alertness, holding very still to avoid detection. Then came decision. The nervous system must put the body into a state of preparedness for action through the outpouring of hormones into the blood, and other processes of the body must be automatically stimulated or inhibited according to need. Action then took place—a fight or an escape, and the process was completed without interference. Like the cat, primitive man then returned to a state of relaxation—of balance.

Great hope for action still lingers in the muscles of civilized man. As in walking, grasping, and chewing, this impulse for action has come down from primitive times. Any stimulation from thinking or emotion awakens it and produces preparation for action in the muscles. If action does not take place, tension lingers and continues as long as the stimulation lasts, and often even longer. Action impulses come from the central reflexes and memory patterns, and are a vital part of our preparedness for danger. They cannot be aborted, although *they can be inhibited* —a destructive way of "self-control."

CHAPTER XVIII

The Role of the Imagination

Imagination is a type of thinking. Memory is another type of thinking. Reasoning is still another type of thinking. Perhaps the most fundamental of these is memory. It is necessary to the survival of all animals. In man only are reasoning and logic supreme. He may build his own pictures in his imagination by admitting or refusing to admit factors bearing upon them. To the degree that he chooses facts wisely he ceases to operate by the "trial and error" method.

"There is no short road to glory," is an old, trite saying, but it is full of truth. Genius is interpreted as the capacity for hard work. We do not all aspire to be geniuses, but a little careful thought need not be hard work unless, by our emotional attitude, we make it so. Often those who have the most need have a "set" against learning. Unless we understand relaxation and its use in the human machinery, we cannot hope to establish it as a daily habit in our lives. Poise and peace in living remain just out of our reach.

Unless the various parts of our living machinery take time *every minute of the day* to refuel and relubricate, our working rhythms are lost. If this loss is temporary we call it functional. Through some emergency of acute strain the deep mechanisms have lost their precise timing in the rhythms of movement. In such a case complete rest restores the human to normal functioning. If one's emotional life is full of manufactured emergencies, the mechanisms which prepare for action are over-wrought and a chronic state of unnecessary preparedness displaces the natural functioning of relaxation in the nerve and muscle connections; their timekeeper is confused and that which would result in a collision on the railroad becomes an explosion in the human machine. This takes many forms of hysteria; we are all acquainted with them. Chronic tension becomes a more or less serious disease. We do not have to travel that road if we will spend a little thought on the use of relaxation in the human economy and how it came to serve in the preservation of life. Our inherited mechanisms, the reflexes, function in the life-saving situation. Throughout the ages they have had plenty of practice and we would still have the full benefit of their functioning if the "intellect" of man had not superimposed many false virtues and artificial interpretations upon our daily thinking.

All thinking is physiological. It requires the physical channels of coordination to produce the evidence of thought. Enlivened as it is by muscular memory, the body is a sensitive instrument responding with a wisdom far surpassing that of man's reasoning or conscious control. What comes in through the pathways of the senses must be organized and come out through the pathways of movement. Through the imagination memory-pictures are organized into patterns of action.

To change our habits of thinking we must know some of the facts involved in our unconscious behavior. We need not pride ourselves on knowing how we behave or on our ability to control our behavior. Two thirds, at least, of our behavior is unconscious, and when we know the facts about it we are completely humbled.

Have you ever given any thought to how your body approaches a piece of work? If the task is to be an agreeable one, you know how you approach it mentally and emotionally: you approach it with interest and as a game, as a child does his play. The activity flows through the imagination with joy and optimism and the physical body picks it up with free motion. The picture of accomplishment is a moving picture in deed and in feeling. Your attention continues to follow the action, to see it as being done, and you have a feeling for it. Your bodily response follows freely when the thinking, the emotion, and the desire to do accompany each other. Relaxation plays its role in every pursuit when these conditions are present. All the bodily mechanisms cooperate for a desirable, optimistic project. The imagination plays upon the picture of accomplishment as "being done." You are your project. There is no separation.

Quite the opposite is true when you dislike your task. There is hesitation, doubt, criticism of self or of the object of the pursuit, and confusion as how to tackle it. Do not fancy that the physical body does not register these objections. There is lack of coordination in the rhythms of movement because of a static condition in the responses, owing to hypertension in the muscles. A poorly executed piece of work and further dissatisfaction! Tensions pile up in the wake of such an experience. Thus habits are built. Either dissatisfaction or satisfaction accumulates conditions in the muscles which make for further dissatisfaction or satisfaction.

UNCONSCIOUS ACTIVITIES

In isolated form, laboratory facts about human behavior remain academic but, assembled, they take shape and meaning in our daily lives. We become what we contemplate. A thought must take form in the thinking before it can flow into behavior. The "form" assembles from our "memory charts" what we have already learned; the action assembles from our emotional habits.

Emotional confusion interrupts clear thinking, and the purposes of the individual are not well defined. Only as patterns of thought flow freely through the imagination can response be effectively organized by the inner mechanisms. It matters not whether the thinking demands bodily movement or abstract calculation: muscular response is involved in both these mental processes.

Unconscious activity is activity of free reflexes in which learning takes place and habits are formed. A man who plays an important part in any historical event or period never realizes its far-reaching significance. The importance of his own contribution does not weigh in his consciousness. If it did he would superimpose upon his actions patterns of behavior foreign to the progression of his original ideas and ideals. His ideas and ideals take form in his imagination and flow through his reflexes into living activity. He is one with his picture. Through imagination and identification he projects his vital purposes. We still learn as a child learns, and through the same mechanisms. These are all facts which are not academic and should not be considered so. They relate to the everyday life of each of us. Only as facts have emotional value do we learn.

A geometric problem, as a parroted statement, means nothing to us, but for a man working out a theorem it has meaning. If he dislikes such work the result is too often unsatisfactory. Unconscious resentments block the easy flow of the inner nerve-mechanisms which must function coordinately to supply the facts needed, at the time needed. Such a man may wake up in the morning with the missing link in his problem clearly in his mind. The release in sleep of his conscious likes and dislikes has allowed his memory patterns to assemble freely in his picture of accomplishment.

IMAGINATION AND IDENTIFICATION

The baby learns through imagination and identification. He first acquires a feeling for the impressions that come to him from the outside world. As soon as he *recognizes a feeling* for a group of impressions, they pass through his imagination and he identifies himself with them. For example, the adults moving about him give him no feeling for walking until he is ready for it. He has already recognized the feelings for food and the conditions in his life which enable him to acquire it. He learns to hold the bottle in his hand and later to handle his spoon successfully. He may also have been conditioned emotionally to know that the baby who cries the loudest gets the bottle. When the child structurally and physiologically is ready for walking, he gets a feeling for it. He watches his elders, and eventually the action of walking passes through his imagination and he identifies himself with it. Walking is accomplished. We do not teach a child to walk. His reflexes respond to his imagination. Impressions from these early emotional and physical conditionings are important. They last throughout life, and affect future behavior.

We are the sum total of impressions, sensations, satisfactions, and dissatisfactions established in thought grooves. This moving picture which you call yourself has been slowly organized throughout babyhood and childhood. Visual images, tactile images, auditory images, emotional images all fall into line to color, time, and arrange your behavior. We live in this inner picture-gallery without analyzing it. We cannot see ourselves for the images—there are too many overlapping. When desire or need calls forth segments of these pictures we find our responses ready and organized for action. These impressions have been coordinated in our imagination to come forth as behavior. We see each act as already done.

SENSE PATHWAYS

From the laboratories of physical science we now learn that, instead of having but five senses, as formerly considered, there are eighteen or twenty sensory responses made through special sense organs. And there are several hundred deviations of these special senses.

There are reports from the sensory nerves in muscles, tendons, and joints or we could not have reflexes controlling, in the unconscious, so many of our actions. An example of this interplay of sensations and response is the "stretch reflex." This reflex enables a joint while engaged in one movement to prepare for the next movement. You bend your knee in walking, but the stretch reflex straightens it for the next step.

Added to the sensation coming from the human framework

are the many organic sensations from heart, digestive tract, reproductive organs, ears, eyes, mouth. These are our physical
"capital" from which we spend according to our desires and
training. Thinking passes through the body parts and comes
out as behavior. But first it becomes organized in the brain and
central nervous system upon receipt of the incoming sensations.
These come from within the body as well as from without.
Something must come in in order for something to come out.
Through the special sense-organs we have received all the information we possess. How this works is exemplified in the
development of the "air sense" which is a part of the aviator's
stock in trade. It results from the organization of many sense
organs whose combined impressions give the feeling of balance,
relaxation, and quick coordination of the body, in response to
the changing positions and situations which must be met by the
pilot in flying.

EARLY YEARS OF TRAINING

In no later five-year period does the individual absorb so
much knowledge as in the first five years of babyhood. His
imagination vitalizes all information for his use. Through identification and imagination he learns. He identifies all knowledge
with himself. He lives a life of story and make-believe entirely
his own. The effects of these early years of experience are with
him throughout life.

As the youth learns, he passes through a talkative stage, a
reticent stage, an egotistical stage; and all this is necessary to
gain powers of speech, courage, and confidence in facing a complicated world. By trial and error he learns many things. If
during a normal life span he succeeds in reaching *maturity*
before he reaches the grave, he will have to be willing to face
facts as they are, to talk less and think more and, most important of all, to have a desire to think straight. In an atmosphere
of truth his ego will have small opportunity to become inflated.

Refusal to answer the child's questions leads him to form
answers to suit his fancy in his imagination. Building facts into
the imagination of the child is the responsibility of the adult;
if his imagination is filled with facts, it won't be filled with

fancies. When fancies lie in the imagination of the child and bring forth untruthful statements, instead of moralizing about falsehoods, guide him with care toward facts. Impatience and punishment only make the problem worse, resulting in inhibitions which may be most harmful. Facts isolated from the whole may become a part of the fancies or "daydreams" in the imagination, distorting future behavior by their lack of relationship to the whole personality and to the environment. In the adult these unrelated facts, broken off from the whole, may produce systematized delusions which in the extreme we call paranoia.

There are many border cases among us in which the "delusions" vary only in degree. Delusions are caused by cutting off facts from the whole and forming an artificial system of thinking in a dream world. The patterns in the imagination are followed by action. Systematized delusions become real. Self or personality is the medium through which we meet our world, and our habitual attitudes are the pictures of ourselves which we daily present to our fellows. Actions flow through our imagination into behavior. The imagination is the tool of the scholar as well as of the paranoiac. Since most of our behavior is unconscious, what our imaginations feed upon is important.

IMAGINATION IN LEARNING

Learning in the adult, as well as in the child, comes through the imagination. After information enters the cortex and reasoning accepts it, it must pass into the imagination for correlation and response. Otherwise we do not learn. We see each act as already done, or picture each step in the formation of a new concept.

Facts in the imagination are the avenue through which all education must enter the reflexes. Correlation may form a new concept or stimulate an immediate muscular response. If the imagination is not fed with facts, but with notions and fancies, it is filled with confused issues having no relation to the whole. The cultivation of constructive, factual pictures for our imagination to feed upon is the wisest thing we can do. This is accomplished through our daily mental and emotional habits.

When we deal with facts and with action we build a positive personality.

If you think, "I cannot succeed," you are working on a plane of failure. We must eliminate negative expressions such as, "I cannot see myself doing so and so," and, "It is useless for me to try that." We should avoid these expressions, not only in their application to our own state of being, but also in our analyses of the conditions of other persons and things. It is easy to recognize factual thinking in the constructive personality. It is equally easy to recognize fictional, notional thinking in the negative personality.

It is distressing to hear a self-styled "practical person" offer the information that he has *no imagination,* that he only deals with *facts.* He would not be so proud to state that the biceps of his right arm was atrophied and henceforth he would be unable to play games.

Imagination plays a great part in our conscious integration, in our learning process. The receiving ends of our nerves bring us impressions which we can recall as visual images, verbal images, and images related to all other senses. These repeat themselves and have an effect upon our current images, although rarely do they separate themselves in consciousness. If we tried to separate these many messages in our waking hours, we could take little pleasure in our surroundings, as the past would be too everlastingly present.

This awareness is true of the learning process on all planes. Physiologically, the growth and inner functioning must be present, the memory pathways must be free, and the "desire to do" must act as the driving force. All this integrated in the imagination! When these conditions are active, coordination and learning take place; new pictures can be formed, new movements executed. Imagination is the life of personality.

Encourage the imagination. Consciously recognize its use and keep it flexible throughout life. Positive, constructive thinking is thus fostered, and negative, abortive thinking discouraged. The alertness of youth will thus replace the atrophy of age.

Work and play should be the same in physical response. It

is our emotional and mental state that makes the difference between them. The body loves activity, gives itself to it with joy when the mental attitude is free. If we establish a philosophy of rest through balance, activity can be free in both work and play.

IMPORTANCE OF IMAGINATION TO THE CHILD

The following true story exemplifies the interplay of identification and imagination of the child. It clearly shows the part played by this interplay of personality and accomplishment.

A young mother had great difficulty with her highly imaginative child whenever she had to face the ordeal of taking her on a bus. Before they could get on, there was always this request, "Mama, let me get my children on first—Tony, Santa, Elvira, Alice, Mae—there, they are all on." Mother in the meantime was pushing her little girl gently to appease the impatient conductor, while she smiled apologetically at the other passengers waiting to board the bus.

The climax came one day when it happened that there remained a vacant seat next to the child. The bus stopped at a corner. A very robust lady took the vacant seat. Instantly, wails rent the air, surprising everybody, who saw the little girl bury her face in her mother's lap. Mother, patting her gently, asked what was the matter. To the astonishment of all listening ears, this burst forth: "The big lady sat down on my husband!"

Soon the child was made happy and comfortable by a few more pats from mother, and a winning smile and kindly word from the "big lady," who moved over a wee bit to make room for the imaginary husband. And the little "wife" and "mother" was serene and happy.

The right handling of children largely determines their future. With blame and inhibition, confusions arise and learning is thwarted. Praise or blame builds into the child his ideal of himself. A balance between these two is required for an integrated personality.

Activities within the child—in muscles, glands, nerves, brain cells, and even vital organs—are constantly conditioning and reconditioning his response patterns. The spoken words and the responses of elders form a part of his mosaic of behavior. The danger lies in suppressing instead of guiding the fabrications and activities of imagination which are the outcroppings of his inner picture. Imagination is the most important process in the child's life. To thwart it, ignore it, or brush it aside is damaging. When a pattern of movement is thwarted it tends to become prolonged, to persist rather than to break up and resolve, as it would have if movement had taken place. Social amenities do not allow us to strike or run, kick or scream when we are angered, afraid, worried, or anxious. But our methods in refraining from such responses may result in a great repression of movement and a damming up of our vital forces.

Willingness to search for and find the truth, whether agreeable or disagreeable, is the mark of an intelligent person. It takes courage to dispute tradition in favor of truth. To seek facts behind the Ivory Door in the face of strong legendary grip of his people took a king indeed, as so beautifully and subtly depicted by Milne in his exquisite play, *The Ivory Door*.

DAILY USE OF THE IMAGINATION

Only by free expression do we utilize all our powers. Only as we utilize our powers do we grow in power. That is, only by thinking do we improve our thinking; only by writing do we improve our writing; by playing tennis our tennis game; by golf our golf game. We can learn the art of swimming in the wintertime and skating in the summer by the use of the imagination to get a feeling for the movements we are learning. When we put them into actual practice the learning process will be partly accomplished.

We each have an imagination but some are more conscious of its use than others. Recalling dreams is difficult for some and yet we all have dreams. We can cultivate the ability to recall them. We can also cultivate the ability to recognize and to use the imagination. The facts that every individual dreams and every individual has an imagination have been utilized in the analysis and interpretation of human behavior. Learn more about the use of your own imagination.

After reading this book and learning where and how your individual weights sit, hang, or are braced, test the use of the imagination in easing the bodily strain in daily activities. For example: reduce the muscular tensions while driving a car by imagining a twenty-five-pound weight dragging on each elbow, and while doing this sit very deep in the pelvic bones as though the spine were sinking through them into a quicksilver bed. This sinking of the pelvis will produce a suction upon the thighs, drawing them back into the body. This will form a very acute angle at the thigh joints and you will have freer ankle-action at the accelerator.

While slowly motoring, frequently carry through these pictures and note the reduction of fatigue at the end of the day. Driving a car with the knees and elbows pulls the spine out of balance and the end result is tense neck- and shoulder-muscles, as the head must keep balanced for eye focus no matter how the spine is pulled from under it. After you have learned to think through your bones instead of in your muscles, a little practice in these procedures while driving slowly will soon give you a different technique of driving and greatly reduce the strains and tensions.

The imagination will organize all muscles to change balance, if you will trust it. Picture how weight should travel through the bones—the muscles will take care of the adjustments.

Many typists, as well as motorists, operate their machines from elbows and knees instead of balancing the body so that all muscles are free.

The spine controls all movements of arms and legs, standing or sitting, and it is wise to draw the legs back toward the spine frequently and let the arms hang straight down heavily from the shoulders and neck. The typist, like the pianist, should avoid playing the keys from the elbows. It produces deep tensions and great fatigue.

The imagination will work for you if you encourage it.

CHAPTER XIX

Pathways of Learning

We are considering an organism which, asleep or awake, is constantly receiving messages from its environment and reacting to them. Its responses are mainly automatic, determined partly by stimuli which lie within the organism making ready for response.

Our acquaintance with our world comes to us through the receiving nerves, inner as well as outer ones. All that we know and feel enters through these avenues. Through hearing and sight, however, come our greatest stimuli for acquiring learning and developing judgments leading to increased intelligence.

In the unconscious wisdom of the ages lie our mechanisms for learning. The velocities and the directions they take in the learning process are important to the growing individual. If they turn inward, the velocities may be increased instead of diminished. The "inferiority complex" or the "unsocialized attitude" result from negative response through forced inhibition. Energy turned in, to break out later in behavior patterns! These may be very definite and even predictable.

INTERMINGLING OF INNER AND OUTER STIMULI

Life is a continuous flow of actions and reactions, all of which are registered within the individual. This is true not only of man's daily actions and reactions, but of those of his ancestors before him. Survival patterns of behavior have been building in the inner man for millions of years. This wisdom has been submerged, drifted under, by social inheritance, which has blocked the primary stimuli and our recognition of them. Hence the wisdom of the "inner man" cannot operate freely. In every living person there are survival patterns and patterns of racial inheritance. These are important antecedents of all thinking and doing. Something cannot start from nothing!

Stimuli, inner and outer, condition and recondition our learning. The extent and value of such learning depends, however, on receptivity and coordination, and the desire to evaluate and use that which is being received. Outer stimuli are influenced by inner stimuli organized from the past. The inner stimuli include our *social* inheritance—prejudices, notions, and predispositions—protected by fixed grooves of thought and action, hedged by "walls" (organized standards) erected during social evolution. Individuals so conditioned can never discover truths that come by increasing the range of reception, can never know poise through directed impulses toward known ends, unmoved by superstitions and freed from prejudices. The wisdom of the inner man must break through these "walls" if further growth is to be accomplished. Acquainting ourselves with the underlying intelligence of the inner man will give us a starting-point in reconditioning our behavior for more successful living than we have thus far attained.

Man becomes more and more educated as observations from without are more finely coordinated with memory patterns within and adequate responses are made. It is our business to realize this activity and not to block or distort it by *fictional ideas* in the imagination, unrelated to the whole.

Whatever the sensory stimulus, the organism responds as a whole. The highly specialized receptors perform the functions for which they are prepared; but once the stimulus is received, it embarks upon a course that may arouse every cell in the organism to appropriate response. The organism as a whole kicks a football, jumps over a fence, eats sukiyaki, runs from a bear, or smells a rose. This is the scientific as well as the common-sense view of man's organized responses. A very important aspect of intelligence in the living organism is the ability to correlate speedily the reports received from the farflung empire of sense. The speed of man's responses and the directions they take lie in the wisdom of his inner velocities and the intelligence of his choices.

Education is not a receptive process. The stimuli received must be coordinated. This is a cooperative, active process of the whole organism. Education requires interpretation of that which is being received and an understanding of its meaning in relation to the whole.

Man as a receiving, correlating, and responding organism is to be evaluated by the things to which he is sensitive, the orderliness of his correlations, and the quality of his responses. Let a person begin to regard himself as this sort of organism, as a dynamic man, and he has taken the first step toward the command of his forces.

ATTENTION AND LEARNING

Paying attention is difficult to learn. One may note how few people, even among adults, have really achieved it. It has been demonstrated that one's span of attention is an infinitesimal period of time. That which we call "concentration" consists of numerous separate, distinct impulses of attention, similar to the impulses of electric discharges over a transmission wire. We speak of a flow of electricity, a flow of thought; it seems a "flow" to our senses because the time element involved in the discharges or impulses is not discernible to us.

When we succeed in directing our attention we have mastered the faculty of concentration. When the attention is directed, observations are made. We see more, hear more, and generally discern more about the objects engaging our attention. More and more facts come to light to add to our memory charts, and be integrated later through the imagination, into behavior patterns.

MIND

What is your "mind"? How does your mind seem to you? You may say that the mind is something in you that can think, for if you think there must be something to do the thinking, and that would surely be the "mind."

In the light of our present knowledge we can no longer think of "mind" as an individual entity, located in a particular place—cortex, heart, stomach, brain: organs which have been credited as being the "seat of mind" in past history. We now know that brain, nerve, and muscle activity are inseparable. One does not act without the other. Mind and matter can no longer be divorced but must be studied as different phases of a single vital and incredibly complicated situation. We should conceive of the "mind," then, not as a thing that does something, but as a name for things that we perceive to be happening. Thinking objectified!

What is thinking? Is it remembering, planning, judging, believing, doubting, wishing, feeling? Each of these activities has a physiological basis, coordinated within an organism which has had millions of years of practice. Thinking, therefore, is the name of a process. We think with the whole body; it is receiving, correlating, responding. Stimuli comes through the senses, and in the process of coordination the whole body is active in thinking; all its systems cooperate in this activity.

LEARNING INVOLVES MOVEMENT

What is meant by "mental and bodily"? Does it mean what goes on in the brain as against what goes on in the body? Scientists offer abundant proof that brain and muscle activity are inseparable. Although *visible* contractions of muscles are not a necessary part of the thinking, thought is a stimulating experience and muscles respond unerringly to stimulation.

The interaction of what we call bodily changes and mental operations is beyond the imagination of the most keen-eyed observer. But it is evident that bodily and mental states are never dissociated. *We cannot think a thought without a muscle change.*

Activity is the law of life. Intellectual growth results from self-activity. This is spontaneous, subject only to a stimulating and engaging environment. The imagination grows by what it feeds upon. We become what we most frequently think about. The brain ripens by experience and thinking quickens by use. As facts assemble we improve our techniques in physical skills, be they operating on the human eye or solving a problem in calculus. For this there must be freedom for expression, muscular freedom, and emotional desire to do, supported by faith to carry it through.

HOW AND WHY IN LEARNING

"Why" is a query that evokes many diverse responses. These responses depend largely upon the emotional background of the individual answering the query; upon the notions, prejudices, and loosely associated ideas assembled out of past experience. "Why" is looking for a cause. There is no single cause for an act. Without the query "how," causes are difficult to find.

Looking for a cause is like looking for the driving current of a tidal wave. The tidal wave happens because *many conditions,* both near and remote in the total situation, have united to produce it. Our present-day scientists may recognize the many conditions pointing to such a catastrophe, and sound warnings. Communities of human beings wise enough to establish an opposing set of conditions may prepare for the disaster, but cannot avert it.

With any specific set of conditions, chemical, physical, mechanical, certain things are bound to happen. When conditions are ripe the event takes place. This profound fact determines more of man's actions than he is usually willing to admit. The individual likes to feel that he deals directly with the forces and not that the forces deal with him; that his conscious actions are always causal; that he produces the causes. He seldom realizes that his actions are conditional and that he consciously only shares in the conditions. His is often a small share, at that!

Every situation should be considered as a process rather than as a fact. In nature all is movement. *How* it works, then, becomes the important thing to find out. There are many causes, never one only, for any seemingly isolated behavior in either the animate or inanimate.

As man grew in intelligence he began to develop the ability to manipulate those things nearest him and to talk about them with his fellow creatures. He then began to ask the "how" of things instead of the "why." How do clouds form? How does the rain fall? How does fire burn? How does a flying ball stay in the air? How does the swimmer stay afloat? As soon as he began to ask the "how" of things, he began to acquire better command of his own forces in adaptation to his environment.

From these humble beginnings came the body of science as we know it today. The question, "how does it work?" is the keystone of all knowledge. Observation of how anything works produces tangible and constructive conclusions. "Why" may often have destructive answers through careless responses.

"How," used in the vocabulary of a child, encourages constructive education, constructive deductions. His constant query of "why," if not adequately answered, often promotes an increasing resistance within the child to the behavior of things and people in his environment. He becomes less factual and objective in his thinking. Thus emotional inhibitions are favored, confusions arise. Emphasis on the "how" leads to *factual thinking* and further understanding.

LEARNING AS A PROCESS

The man who shall realize his ideal is the one who has the understanding to interpret it and to keep it clear in the imagination. The response will thus become organized.

If you have the ideal, for example, to draw a perfect circle, you must see the circle circling. When the stage is properly set for action—the desire to move, the pencil poised loosely in fingers and resting upon the paper, arm and body free for response—the neuromuscular units will so coordinate the pattern of movement through arms and fingers that it will carry through. Your full mental, physical, and emotional cooperation is involved. The circle circles itself onto the paper.

We have seen children apply will power with a sense of duty to their art lessons, tensely holding the pencil, trying to *make it* somehow get that thing on paper. In this situation it is easy to see that no thought of movement is in the thinking, just the need of getting a set form on paper—static, not dynamic. All grip, no flow! If the imagination does not organize the picture in motion, the right motion does not take place.

The full volition must express itself in the desire for movement. Success requires emotional as well as mental content. This opens up the pathways. You must start at a given point, go in a given direction and, in the case of the circle, return to your starting-point. In other words, you must imagine a circle circling and go with the pattern of motion.

What grows in the imagination will come forth in behavior. What lies in the subjective will come out in the objective. Facts and fancies must be kept well separated for understanding and growth in objective living. We must encourage constructive positiveness in our imagination for growth in personality to be possible.

Know what you want, decide where you are going, and all the inner highways and byways for learning open up. This positive assurance of plan acts much the same upon the inner man as the appearance of a well-poised person does upon the outer world. Emerson wisely said, "The world turns aside for the man who knows whither he is going." Know what you want and how you want it. The inner machinery for learning and motion is at your disposal. It will operate!

THE USE OF EMOTION

Emotion is a tool of the primary instincts, the instincts of fear, hunger, rage, sex, all essential for survival of the individual and the race. Thinking is a tool for the emotions. When emotions are blocked, more thinking must take place. When emotions overflood man, his only safe recourse is to redirect his thinking into activity unassociated with the emotion. Efforts to inhibit emotion only strengthen it, do not eliminate it. Thinking cannot control emotions. To be an effective tool for the balance of the emotions, thinking must redirect activity and thus dull the unfavorable by replacement with other emotional satisfactions. So thinking becomes an effective tool for the emotions and for living.

Thinking itself has many tools. First there must be reception through the senses. Then the innumerable stimuli must be evaluated. Reception and evaluation are constantly overlapping. Memory, both hereditary and current, logic, and reason take part in evaluating and building the stimuli into a concept. Then come acceptance and desire to use, before the concept can become activated through the imagination. In activation, coordination takes place through the reflexes. Muscular response of some type is the *final and only* expression of that which is received through the senses. Only by what one does or says can another have any idea either that he is thinking or of what he is thinking. Movement is the full expression of life! Movement becomes more intelligent as factual thinking becomes established in the individual.

The sooner we learn to interpret frankly our own behavior on the basis of facts that influence it, the sooner we shall be able to think intelligently about the social and scientific world which changes so rapidly about us. We must adjust through learning and facing facts, or be submerged.

FACTUAL THINKING

Ability to think grows, as do muscles, with use, not disuse. Logical thinking is an acquired skill. It is hard work and many avoid it when they can. It burns much energy.

Thinking is talking to oneself. In fact, the very process of thinking is dual. "Shall we or shan't we?" "Is it or isn't it?" Thus we temporarily accept, weigh, and evaluate. Silence is necessary for this, also time—time to get a feeling for the facts we are thinking about and to focus them into daily experience. New conclusions through understanding will surely result, new "trials," but fewer "errors." Instead of brute force, thinking should become the life-saving device. Brain versus brawn!

Thinking functions in two ways; objectively, noting par-

ticulars about the changes taking place in an object observed—
in other words, recognizing the stimuli received; and subjec-
tively, in arranging these observations in an orderly fashion in
the form of a mental picture. Both of these functions are physiological. Our nervous mechanisms must receive the stimuli and
do the correlating. The organism, in short, receives myriad
messages and then, on the basis of past experiences, proceeds
to organize itself with respect to them. Muscular responses and
new concepts result.

The transfer of stimuli from one part of the body to another through the neuromuscular paths in response to ideation
or imagery is an involved process, but fortunately it is effected
automatically when the right mental stimulus and emotional
"set" are provided.

In playing a part, the actor first forms a mental concept of
the character he is to depict, and gets a feeling for it. He then
creates the impression he wishes to give, largely through his
bodily attitudes, which react automatically to the stimuli from
his concept. The effective mechanism works through the central
reflexes and the imagination serves to motivate the concept.
Emotional optimism carries through the picture. It is the same
optimism that we use every day at our noonday meal or in
climbing a flight of stairs. Through the imagination we learn;
but we must accept the facts assembled by the cortex, the seat
of reasoning power.

POSITIVE PERSONALITY

Man's command of himself and his environment grows
apace. We see this in the development of a successful person as
he gives and gets more in his interplay with people and events
in his life. His vision becomes sharpened, his moods fewer, and
his power to meditate greater. He is freer from predispositions
and prejudices, and his intelligence accepts the universe and
what it has to offer him in the findings of science and the vast
expressions of the forces of life.

The vast and the minute hold secrets for the man reaching
out for understanding. Such a man has climbed the heights and

sounded the depths. Vicariously he has lived through the cycle of evolution and can commune silently with all ages and all societies. Less ego here, better understanding; continual growth and evolution! We can recall men and women who fit into this picture to the great service of all mankind.

ESSENTIAL RESEARCH

False education has robbed man of the bodily freedom and ease he experienced in his primitive life. If he is ever to attain again his structural balance and relaxation, release from strain and tension, efficiency in his work and play, he must understand the use of his imagination. He must prove for himself that structural and mechanical facts (not opinions or hazy notions) when entertained in the imagination will condition and recondition his neuromuscular habits for an increasing degree of efficiency and ease in living.

When man puts as much factual thinking into the balance and use of his body as he does into the construction of his automobile, the answers to many of his present-day "slowdowns" and "breakdowns" will no doubt come to light.

When a sufficient number of researches have established the correlation between energy consumption and mechanical balance of bodily parts for best support and movement, other objective research can be done to correlate structural balance and function with emotional moods. Many of the answers to the problem of human tension and its meaning in our lives may thus be found.

THE CHALLENGE OF THE PRESENT

The industry of rearing and educating the next generation has never presented the challenge that it does at the present time because of the changes wrought by science in every department of living. We have greater resources than ever before, and the tools created by science give us greater power for constructive or destructive use. Unless we can control the forces at our disposal, they threaten to engulf us.

If there is to be a new recovery in world troubles, we must incorporate into our thinking and into our experience the facts contained in our body of science. Also, we must organize and strengthen such faith as we may have acquired from our particular type of religion. Since science is the study of God's procedures in His universe, would it not follow that science carried to the ultimate would find God in everything? Men and the sick world need facts and faith. National recovery, or world recovery, is a multiple of individual recoveries.

CHAPTER XX

Roads to Greater Ease

Among man's tools for living, those things which lie deepest in his unconscious mechanism, in the reflexes, in the organizers for movement, are the most difficult for him to understand. They function automatically when the imagination is vitalized.

Logic plays no direct part in behavior responses, only in passing accepted facts into the imagination, and in the faculty of inhibition. No *direct* self-volitional efforts can organize a movement. All movement is organized in the imagination, pictured as already done. The age-old unconscious mechanisms carry it through.

We often speak of "imaginary thinking" and "logical thinking." This is a false distinction between "fictional thinking" and "factual thinking." Either must be passed into the imagination to hold any value in active living.

To note how the imagination enlists muscle action, observe the muscles of the nose and mouth of a person watching a friend in sorrow or joy, or looking sympathetically at a child or adult taking a dose of bitter medicine. Note also that it is his face muscles that respond to his imagination, not his toes or fingers.

On the other hand, toes and fingers would respond quickly if the child were about to turn a lighted match toward his face or hair.

If you decide to talk, more things than your tongue have to be prepared. If you are going to use hand or foot, their actions must take form in your imagination, or how could the many exchanges within the nervous system be able to organize intelligently for location, and for the timing and energy needed for precise direction of movement?

Imagination is the one avenue through which the unconscious mechanism controlling velocity, time, and direction of movement in space can be engaged effectively and economically. Imagination is the tool for reconditioning neuromuscular habits. It served us well before "intellectual" man placed it in the criminal class. Facts, not notions, in the imagination are the activating factors through which all true education must enter the reflexes. These facts come from the "department of logic," where they have been accepted, in the frontal brain. The pictures in the imagination must then carry them into action.

Reclaim the imagination. Understand that it is a vital part of the thinking process of man, as well as of the child. By its means learning and relearning take place. All activities must be visualized into reality.

It is well to put into action some form of relaxation before trying to correct tensions while engaged in daily pursuits. Assuming unsocialized positions occasionally is a valuable experience when trying to locate your weight-bearing parts and their true relationships. Positions that have no moral or social claims for themselves encourage more accuracy in the sensory reports. Since such positions have no relation to habitual attitudes, the truth about the positions of parts of the body and how they relate to each other will be discerned more easily. Unsocialized positions, such as lying down on hard surfaces, or the four-legged position, offer another important factor—the change in the pull of gravity on body parts. In these positions gravity passes through the bones in a different direction because they are in a changed relation to the ground. This promotes better balance in muscle action around each joint. Unusual positions should, therefore, be assumed frequently.

BACK-LYING POSITION FOR CONSTRUCTIVE REST

A position most favorable for balanced relaxation is that of lying on the back on a level surface, such as the floor, window-seat, or table. None of these will adjust, as a bed would, to your "too prominent" parts produced by tension. Avoid the bed! Put blankets or rugs under you if you wish, but place them on a level, ungiving surface.

Lie down on your back, bend the knees and thigh joints to draw the feet into parallel position on the floor (toeing in slightly), and bring them as close to the ischia (sit-bones) as is comfortable. Place the arms across the chest so that the *lower* arms lie parallel, with the elbows in line with the thigh joints. Have a pillow if you wish, its size depending on the strains in your neck; at least a slight lift under the head is helpful.

Note where your bones hit the hard surface with the greatest amount of pressure. These points of pressure are caused by tension in the muscles and will change as muscular antagonizers become balanced and relaxation is attained.

Take a mental trip through your bony framework in this *rest position.* Locate and visualize in your imagination the exact place where your head connects with the top of the spine; where the spine attaches to the sacrum. Locate your thigh joints by spanning these joints at the front of the pelvis, a hand-span apart. Note where your ischia are in relation to the end of your spine and in relation to your thigh joints. You can feel their sharp tuberosities. Next note how your knees and ankles relate to each other and to the thigh joints. They should all be in alignment; that is, in the same plane. It is through the action of these joints—ankle, knee, and thigh—that the weight of the spine is balanced and counterbalanced by their upward thrust. They counter all blows from the earth.

Locating your strategic joints is somewhat similar to the

use of a road map. You pick out certain points through which you wish to travel, follow lines of direction over prescribed highways, and make out for yourself your itinerary. You could now fold your map and in your imagination proceed to take your journey. If a friend inquired about your trip, you could indicate on a blank paper your points of greatest interest and the lines of direction necessary to include them all in the imaginary map of your journey. You have formed an integrated picture of specific locations and definite lines of direction. Your desire to travel through this particular pathway makes it possible for you to reproduce your map on a piece of blank paper. The facts in your thinking and the emotional desire work together in your imagination.

So it is with the human body. If you see the value of bone balance and of muscle release, you will think vividly of where the bones sit, hang, or are braced. With this in the imagination small centering movements can be made around joints, and thus the integration of the bony framework will become a reality if your desire is great enough.

Vivid pictures in your imagination of the location of important weight-bearing joints of the body will stimulate the muscle antagonizers to change for better balance. To state it differently: visualizing the exact location of a part—a bone—to be moved, a definite direction for its movement, and the continuation of its movement, will result in better balance of reciprocal muscles around the bone or joint.

LOWERING THE CENTER OF GRAVITY

The center of gravity of any mechanism is lowered as its weight is brought nearer its centerline and nearer its base. When the animal faces danger his preparation mechanisms become active to make him ready for expanded movement. One of these mechanisms is the deep-seated growl or hiss. This serves to warn his enemy but, more important still, it serves as an aid in lowering his center of gravity. It stabilizes his stance and frees his upper structures for active forward movement.

Both the growl and the hiss use deep inner muscles not employed in ordinary exhalation. We cannot go about growling, but we can imitate the hiss of the cat or snake with beneficial results. When first tried it may seem silly—but it works! It relaxes. Try it. It centralizes the weights hanging on the spine.

Force the air out through partly closed teeth and lips, but with lips inactive. The noise should be like the sound of "sssss" continued as long as possible. We sometimes hear this type of sound in registered disapproval of an audience for a speaker at a public gathering. The value of the hiss lies in continuing it, slowly and lazily and *without a break,* as long as possible on one expiration.

The hiss employs deep throat and body-wall muscles which tend to lengthen the thoracic cavity by reducing the lateral diameter of the rib-case. As upward pulls on the spine are reduced, its lumbar region becomes more closely integrated with the diaphragm, transversalis, and deep pelvic muscles. These cooperate in their activity.

One of the inherent qualities of muscle is that by which it prepares for its next contraction the moment it is stretched. As hissing continues the ribs are closed inward and downward, and the circumferential border of the diaphragm with them. Thus the diaphragm is stretched a sufficient amount to promote its complete and strong contraction on the next intake of breath. The stretching of the diaphragm borders is facilitated also by the contraction of the transversalis, which contracts on exhalation. This changes the action of the circulation throughout the body.

THE FOUR-LEGGED POSITION

If man, the biped, could return to the four-legged position, it would be interesting to note how long it would take him to regain that snug cylindrical wall which gives to his brother animal such body compactness.

Man has foreshortened his back wall and extended his front wall to the detriment of the central tubular cylinder containing his vital organs. You can become aware of this by standing on your hands and knees and imagining a heavy weight on your back, such as a child piggy-back style, or a pile of books at the waistline. Walk backward, then forward a few steps in a straight line in this position. If you continue to support the imaginary weight, you cannot become "sway-back" like the pony in disrepute on the farm. The back and the front of the body must remain parallel if you walk in a straight line and still support the weight. A few attempts at this will help to integrate the inner supporting muscles of the pelvis at the lumbar spine. The pelvic rim and the sternum should be in the same relationship when you are standing erect and the spinal axis fully as long as when you are on all fours. This is a good way to test your poise and balance when standing.

While on all fours imagine your body a baked Idaho potato. Watch the mealy contents within the skin shrinking inward toward center until the covering becomes as loose as a puppy's skin. Now try walking forward, then backward without breaking the potato skin. This is an amusing little game, but it works and you will feel more relaxed when you get up from your four-legged position. Walking backward and forward, without allowing the abdominal wall to stretch, integrates all the body-wall muscles.

EASE IN SITTING

If you sit long hours at a time your design of body forces will take on a steady drive into elbows and knees. One group of the reciprocal muscles is doing hard work while the opposing groups have too little to do. Static tensions result. Reverse this action frequently through the day and you will relax more easily at night. Learn bone balance in sitting and then practice it often during busy hours.

In trying to find bone balance while sitting, choose a hard, straight chair. Sit as far back as you can. Locate your ischia. Sit on them. Draw your thighs back into their sockets, making an acute angle at the thigh joints. This is done by a sort of suction action at the thigh joints, not by *moving* the legs. Be sure that no weight is driving forward into the knees to press downward upon the feet. Your weight is supposed to travel evenly through the *four legs of the chair* to the floor.

Notice where your back pushes hardest against the back of the chair; shrink around the spine from the neck to the pelvis, drawing the ribs and all parts of the body inward toward the spinal column. The spine controls all, and will pass the weight of all parts downward to the ischia when you are balanced. Shrink!

If you are not balanced in the spine, but various parts are pulling away from it, you will find yourself delivering a goodly share of your weight to the back of the chair at the shoulders, and to the front of the chair at the knees. Often shoulders pressing at the back, and the thighs pressing on the chair seat in front, brace against each other. Why keep working needlessly when sitting? With your center of gravity too high, muscles of the spine are not free to guide the weight through the vertebrae, the joints of support. The *compression* members of your body, the spinal and pelvic bones, cannot serve their designed purpose.

To help re-establish weight in the ischia a few simple movements may be done. While you keep the spinal axis straight and long and your thighs at acute angles with the pelvic rim in front, lift the shoulders straight up toward the ears. Lift and lower them several times in line with the lateral axis of the body. Hiss the breath out between the teeth while doing this. Continue for three long hisses. Lift one foot and then the other from the floor without rocking on the ischia. Repeat shoulder-raising and hissing. Relaxation results.

Stand, then sit again and repeat. If this is done thoughtfully and carefully, you should be able to rotate the entire trunk about the spine in a very free manner *under the shoulder girdle.*

Learn to produce action independently in your spine to aid you in more-centralized control of the extremities. The Indian dancer, Uday Shan-Kar, amused and interested his American audiences by circular movement of the head, controlled deep in the spine. His shoulders seemed to float in space without engaging in the movement.

In your imagination travel down the spine, but do not visualize it merely as a string of bones; think of it as alive and active and completely covered with muscles like your arm or leg. It is longer than your arm, and as large and compact as your leg. It controls the head, the ribs, and all that lies below them. Live with it! Use it consciously. Especially when sitting, help it to hold you straight. Think through it and it will do more work for you.

The first step in conservation of energy and in avoidance of fatigue is to rely upon the law of gravity and trust one's bones to it. Let them sit directly upon, or hang directly under, or rest firmly against, their points of support. Each bony unit has a function to fulfill in a finely adjusted mechanism. Only as bones are aligned for proper function can muscles be relieved of unnecessary work. This relaxes them.

THE PROBLEM OF STANDING

Standing is perhaps the most difficult activity for the inner mechanisms to control. It is a *skill* few of us accomplish with ease. It is to be avoided when possible. Any expansive movement is far more economical.

When obliged to occupy a limited space in the upright position over a long period of time, center the loads frequently. Take a step forward or backward and shift weight (but almost imperceptibly) from one foot to the other.

The most difficult thing in this position is to find the balance and most economical carriage of the spinal weight through the pelvic base and through the rotary joints into the thighs. One finds oneself "setting" the pelvis instead of thinking of it as a swinging basket between two uprights—the spine delivering the body weight and the legs receiving it.

The following must be kept clear in the imagination: the spine supports and controls all body weights; the weight is delivered by the fifth lumbar vertebra to the sacrum at the back; it travels forward to the thighs at the front. One mechanical fact must be added: all forces in the back of the trunk are compression forces and all in the front are tensile forces. All body weights travel down the back—all parts of the front of the body *hang*. The pelvis itself is suspended at the front from high up in the spine via the *iliopsoas* muscles. Think down the back and up the front.

These facts present a simple picture of the pelvis suspended between three movable points—the two thigh joints in the front and the lumbosacral joint in the back. But the adjustment problem is not quite so simple. Because of the compression forces operating at the back, we must give our attention to the tensile forces at the front to be able to *counter* the load with success.

We must first realize that the pelvis should never be *held in a fixed position.* It is a swinging cantilever receiving weight at one end and passing it not to one but to two movable structures at the other end. Keep the tensile members (muscles) on the inside of the pelvis and inner thighs contracting so as to maintain snug bone-contacts of the two thigh joints. In other words, narrow the pelvis at the front and lift it at the front. This effectively directs the axes of upward thrust through the thighs at the front, toward the center of the sacrum at the back. This adjustment will be aided by thinking of weight being delivered to the foot just behind the inner part of the ankle joint, with minimum weight on the great toe. Deliver the weight to the foot toward the *heel end* of the foot.

WALKING DEVICES

To break up habitual imbalances of support and control of body weights and bring back control to central muscles and structures, *unusual positions and movements* must be tried. The familiar ones will bring no sensations of contacts. We must acquire the sensations by changed arrangements. In habitual positions and motions the sensory reports have been dulled. Get acquainted with joint relationships through new positions and adjustments.

There are several devices that can help us walk with greater freedom and ease. The first of these is to see the picture of bone balance and relationships clearly in the imagination; the second is to have a sensory appreciation of when and where we tense muscles. All muscles around the hip bones and thigh joints must be kept free and active to allow the inner muscles, suspending the front of the pelvis and thighs from the spine, to be powerful in their action.

To get a feeling for this freedom of parts unaccustomed to relaxation, walk on a sandy beach, in depth of water to the middle thighs or slightly higher; walk against the current, middle-thigh deep, in any stream; walk through a field thickly carpeted with fallen leaves. If you cannot actually do these things, imagine them as you walk any place. Your picture will activate changes in the parts. You must change the pelvic balance to a free swinging one if you are going to deal successfully with the pressure of moving water or plowing through dry leaves which would come upon the front of the ankles.

Walk backward across a long room toward a blank wall and note which part of your body touches the wall first. Stand in this position, but without forcing any part backward. Now imagine your spine growing downward, long like a dinosaur's tail, until it makes a third leg to support the weight of your trunk. After concentrating on this active picture for a few moments, note whether the pressure of your pelvis against the wall is any lower than it was. It should be higher and lighter.

To encourage a better sense of spinal control in the balance of thighs and pelvis, walk slowly up a hill backward, on the ground, not the pavement; take shorter steps than usual and toe in slightly; keep the spinal axis straight and long as you walk. Be ready to sit down on a camp stool at any moment if one should be placed under you from the back. Do not bend at the waistline with each stride—this would mean bending your spinal axis. After walking backward uphill about ten feet, walk down again with short steps, still keeping the spinal axis long.

Add hissing to this game. After about three repetitions your shoulders will seem to be floating on your body, as in fact they should be; the front pelvic rim and deep lumbar spine will be closer to each other if you have carried in your imagination the points given in this picture of movement. A different alignment of your bones and better spinal control will result from this practice. Control will be brought back to centers of support through deep-lying muscles, thus releasing surface antagonizers.

Walk a rail, or imagine it along a carpet seam. See how much easier you can do it if you look straight ahead than if you look where you place each foot. The semicircular canals and otoliths in the ear are confused when the eye does the measuring for them, and your muscles are "thrown out of gear" by the varying distances of the head from the ground. This reminds one of the frequent admonition to the golfer: "Keep your eye on the ball." This gives the inner mechanisms a chance to do their own measuring. Watching the feet will fatigue the organism rapidly. You never see a tightrope walker look at his feet. An interesting experience in balance is that of walking backward on the deck of a ship when it is in motion. When opportunity offers try this for relaxation.

If you experiment in these ways you will find that your center of gravity has lowered and your lumbar spine and thighs are managing your movements with less strain. You are no longer walking with chin and neck. The head itself will be higher and the spine longer. Weight will thus be nearer center and nearer the base. You grow taller by thinking down the spine. Side-pulls on the bones which should be lowering the weight to the ground are thus reduced and the spinal curves released; they assume their full length.

CLIMBING STAIRS

Walk upstairs without inclining the body forward, that is, keep your spinal axis straight in line with the weight-bearing foot until you have placed the climbing foot on the next stair. When ready to take the step keep the spinal axis still straight, aiming the top of your head toward the ceiling until your weight is over the forward foot. This means that the movement of your body will be in the patterns of the stair steps. The axis of the spine and trunk are always *vertical;* they serve best in this plane in climbing. As a further aid, employ again in your imagination the dinosaur's tail, letting it drag on the stairs.

The body is a unit; the muscles moving it must act together upon bony levers to maintain balance. The real necessity is freedom in mechanical action and ease in muscular function. The first is produced by laws of balance; the second by laws governing reciprocal muscle-action for organized movement— laws of pure mechanics and laws of biologic origin working together.

Examples of these laws in action are the pard-like tread of the Indian and the noiseless tread of the family cat climbing the back stairs, his weight propelled from the rear. Note how clumsy and noisy he is, however, when going down stairs. His front limbs are unaccustomed to the control and balance of his body weights. This is a learned pattern. A cat more often comes down from high places, such as treetops, backward. Its *posture reflexes* are *better conditioned* for this procedure.

Try imitating the dog's method of climbing stairs. It will not only change your strains, but with your center of gravity so close to the stairs, the heart, along with your muscles, will appreciate taking it easier. In other words, go up on all fours.

RELAXATION THROUGH MOVEMENT

With a little thought applied to bone balance you may account for your muscular tensions; you can thus determine how to change them. After assuming the rest position lying on a hard surface with knees bent, draw the great toe, without curling it, back toward the heel; draw the thighs back into their sockets and toward the spine within the pelvis, draw the ribs toward the spine as you would fold down an umbrella. Move the shoulders up and down and backward and forward without pushing them with the arms. This unlocks the superficial pulls of muscles and recenters bones. Try hissing as you do the shoulder movement. In fact, use hissing with all advised movements, for it always increases relaxation.

To add further relaxation and circulatory benefits to this position, place the back of the ankle of one foot upon the knee

of the other leg. After being sure that both thighs ;
line with their sockets (the knee of the top one, in ṛ.
may be pointing outward: bring it in), proceed to bend the top
ankle-joint carefully but fully backward and forward *without
moving the knee.* This latter injunction is the most important
one to follow. You may think your foot is doing all the work,
but your spine is controlling to a large extent the steadiness
and direction of foot movement by its muscular connection with
the thigh at its socket and inside of the pelvis. When you can
move the ankle freely *without engaging the knee in movement,*
spinal control of the thigh is attained; the deep muscles of lower
leg and foot are operating on the ankle, and the superficial
muscles are no longer pulling on the knee.

Stand and flex one thigh until it forms a right angle with
the body. With the *knee in line with the thigh socket,* allow the
lower leg to hang straight downward so that the ankle is directly under the knee, toes forward. Now bend the ankle back
and forth. Next swing the lower leg from the knee like a pendulum.

The lower leg must dangle like an empty, wet stocking, so
that it may swing back and forth of its own weight like a pendulum set in motion. Watch the stocking "dry" until you get
the feeling of weight. No conscious knee-action must be present.
When you have acquired sufficient balance in the leg you are
standing on to be able to do this, change legs and repeat with
the other. When each can freely, of its own weight, swing from
the knee, lie down again and do the ankle-bending.

Playing games in the imagination is an easy way to make
habitual the changes that are needed for better bone-balance.
These should be used in various positions and in different
situations.

REST PRECEDES SLEEP

After you go to bed there are several pictures and positions
that will be relaxing. Turn on the side with head on pillow and
the shoulder forward so that you lie on the ribs, not the shoulder. Bend the thighs and knees until they each form right angles
at thigh joints and at knee joints. In this position, make the

back and front body-walls as compact as you can by "shrinking" toward your spine until the contents of your body-wall cylinder are snug within.

From the ischia to the atlas imagine this cylindrical structure so complete in itself that your arms and legs seem merely attached loosely to the outer wall at their joints, like those of a rag doll. Hiss while visualizing this picture, to decrease the lateral diameter of the body wall and thus further integrate the spine and the body contents. About three hisses and you are ready for the next step. With ankles touching each other, bend the feet as far as you can, sharpening the heel downward. This must be done without stirring the knees; without disturbing the right angle at the knee or thigh joints. After sharpening the heel downward, bend the feet backward, stretching the toes, again without movement at the knees. Repeat this three or four times during several hisses. After attaining free ankle-movement, curl the toes several times as you would curl the fingers in closing your fist. Relaxation and changed circulation will result.

RELIEF FROM DISTURBING EMOTIONS

When you feel temper creeping upon you, the use of your muscles in some form of expansive movement is necessary: shadow boxing; lying on your back on the floor and pedalling a bicycle upside down, bumping the knees as you pedal; walking rapidly; running; any rapid work which keeps pace with the inner velocities. These accumulate and must be dissipated through action. The energy ratios must be expended before they turn upon others, or inward upon yourself. Inhibition is to be avoided by *expanded movement*. Balance and relaxation must again be established. Otherwise temper will sooner or later explode, to the harm of yourself and others. Balance and relaxation come only through constructive patterns of movement or *active satisfactory mental employment*.

MAN AND ENVIRONMENT INTERTWINE

Life is a stream of energy, active and purposive, molding and remolding mechanisms to meet the changing environment.

Man is what his environment and heritage has made him. The tools it has offered him have been employed successfully for his survival. As his knowledge and intelligence grow, the application of these tools in his daily living can become more effective.

New feelings as well as new analyses must come about if habits are to be changed. Dr. James Harvey Robinson voiced a great truth when he said, in *The Humanizing of Knowledge,* "Any most familiar object will suddenly turn strange when we look it straight in the face. As we repeat some common word or regard keenly the features of an intimate friend, they are no longer what we took them to be. Were it not for our almost unlimited capacity for taking things for granted, we should realize that we are encompassed with countless mysteries, which might oppress our hearts beyond endurance, did not custom and incuriosity veil the depths of our careless ignorance."

CHAPTER XXI

Fatigue and Rest

Sleep, being a negative phase, cannot be compelled. Consciousness, being a positive phase, can be compelled even unto death. This is a sinister and two-edged comment about fatigue. Its boundaries are so extraordinary that a man may die of it, or may be taken by it far out of the bounds of his familiar self. We too often push ourselves to the nth degree in daily living.

The meaning of fatigue is simplified in the manifestation and therapy of the extremes—shock and exhaustion. Dr. George Crille's premise is that shock and exhaustion are identical. In the acute stage of shock and exhaustion a man, he states, "can see danger but cannot escape, can understand words but cannot make normal response, the organism has lost its self-mastery."

Exhaustion is produced by lack of food, water, air, and sleep; by overexposure, overwork, and emotional strain, as well as by infection. The correction is restoration of physical, chemical, emotional balance.

From the time when clocks were invented, and certainly from the moment when workers began to do for pay in fixed hours what they did not really want to do, they must have carried inertia and begun a rigidity of cumulative fatigue. There is a repetition in fatigue patterns. One does not have to work in a factory to produce the results of pressure methods. Often the reader or thinker holds the tongue tightly, contracts the throat and the jaw muscles, as if in lockjaw. One may move nervously the hands, feet, body, and backbone to no valuable affect; also use too much force in talking, thus throwing a shrill voice from the throat rather than a resonant voice from the diaphragm. Such persons often use two pillows. They rarely abandon themselves to the bed and sleep.

FATIGUE MANIFESTATIONS

Our deeper studies of fatigue are bringing us to the realization that breakdowns are seldom from overwork. They come from overflooding energy which has never been used in balance with environmental needs.

When we acquaint ourselves with our interesting mechanisms we discover that most of our fatigue problems start in the emotional field and are both psychological and physiological. Susceptibility to irritations builds up tensions during fatigue. Anxiety develops impatience.

Two important causes of tension are temper and fear. When we continually inhibit fear and are ashamed of it, we retain the tensions which are the result of natural warnings of danger. Fear when used in an objective expression as caution causes no deep, lasting tensions. Anger, too, is an instinctive reaction which we must watch carefully or it steals upon us and accumulates tension. To the extent that it has not been directed into useful channels of activity in childhood it remains the master of its victim. He never "grows up."

The overfatigued person becomes very persistent about his own particular interests and pursuits and does not like to have his attention diverted to any other pursuits. His range of interests decreases as his fatigue increases. He may even become fanatical over a very simple issue. As he resents interference he is in continuous preparation for something that never arrives. He is "on the verge" all the time, like a person sitting on the edge of a car seat impatient for the engine "to get there!" His very impatience is an aspect of anxiety and fear.

In its high stage, cumulative fatigue has a pattern of restlessness, a state of overmobilized energy, more than the job can use or the person can get rid of. The American metropolis expresses this excess of energy; more power than is used is felt in the air. In the low opposite, fatigue approaches the state of enervation which follows illness or extreme physical exhaustion.

Fatigue is the beginning of that functional disturbance which in time, and with further fatigue, comes to the organic break. With the habit of it comes the *endurance of it,* so that shops fill with and theaters play to groups who are always immoderately tired. They are there to enjoy activities vicariously, hoping that the tensions of the day may be broken.

FUNCTIONAL FATIGUE

The desired normal in fatigue is only a little more than the pleasant tiredness after swimming, walking, or playing a game. That grand and glorious tiredness after pleasurable outdoor activity has something of an exhilaration about it! This is the fatigue that brings the incentive to pause, which then makes new activity welcome. In everyday life, work seems to be a logic of rhythm followed more fiercely in winter than in summer. You contain work, it fills you, you empty yourself of it at the end of a cycle, which may be a day, a week, or longer. It is the completion of the *cycle* that means rest. The continued preparation by body mechanisms for work is over and rest is possible.

So long as fatigue maladjustment remains functional there is always the possibility of applying our intelligence to its correction. However, when the functional rhythm-imbalances continue over a long period without correction, physical and chemical changes may take place in cell structure. We then have an organic instead of a functional disturbance, and the remedy is much harder to find. Intelligence should be applied before it is too late. Fatigue must be interrupted soon enough and often enough to permit recovery by balance and rest.

Never accumulate fatigue. Whatever its causes, it is the antithesis to balanced activity, in which rest is paired with work, as exemplified by all the vital systems of our human economy. The end result of overfatigue is lack of coordination between parts. The products of work, organized movements, are no longer dependable. Mental attention is reduced and emotional excitability or physical lassitude are inevitably present.

FATIGUE POISONS

Since all substance yields it suffers fatigue. Your automobile engine works better after a rest. Structural and molecular balances have been re-established.

In the human being, fatigue is due to waste products. The working balance of the muscles is affected by sarcolactic acid and other wastes. Through the chemical changes in the cells the working muscular rhythm, due to reciprocal muscle-action, becomes unbalanced. The overfatigued muscle may be stiff and slow in response or it may be too rapid and jerky in action.

Breakdown products may serve also as a stimulant for further action. In this phase of fatigue one does not recognize that he is fatigued. Waste products continue to accumulate because of cell depletion and chemical imbalance. They may also accumulate because of psychic factors interfering with muscle rhythms. When rest and activity phases of muscle bundles have ceased a balanced relationship, a condition of continued action, when action is no longer needed, results. One feels he cannot stop.

MODERN LIFE

To guard against the daily overfatigue of modern life, and the tension habits resulting from it, good mental and emotional teamwork should be sought. Try to find the "desire to do" what has to be done. Worry over that "tired feeling" only adds more toxins to the tissues, and further reduces accomplishment. Warnings are always sounded. Learn to interpret and to heed them. Fatigue patterns with static tensions, increased day after day, may persist many weeks without release. They continue even in sleep. Vague shadows stalking the unconscious—making life dull and uninteresting!

Dr. Richard Cabot warned his patients that rest means the removal of abnormal loads and the promotion of normal activity; that they should never accumulate fatigue, but "shift the load" or drop it for a while. *Removal* of loads implies action. Move more, hold less. This applies to the mental as well as to the physical realm. Change the thinking. Release the fixed ideas, the struggle to attain them, as well as fixed bodily positions. Direct the emotional "set" toward accomplishment, not toward establishment of more "sets." Dare to make a mistake, and thus grow. Rectifying a mistake is a step forward. It releases fresh energies.

The two outstanding causes of fatigue are duration of movement and frustration of movement. If we are *fighting within,* the inherited aggressive fighting apparatus responds. The "fight is on," but motion does not take place. Static contractions within muscles, however, are accumulating fatigue poisons. When muscles accumulate fatigue, chemical cellular balance is lost and must be regained.

Over-long muscle contractions without rest, even though imperceptible, pile up and may partake of the nature of "shock." The neuromuscular system, in its effort to deal with the unassimilable stimuli, engages many side chains of reflexes. These increase the muscular strains and confuse the signals. Thus a vicious circle produces further emotional as well as physical imbalance. Fatigue becomes the master.

Balanced bodily rhythms include the resting and working phases. The heart is a very good example of frequency of resting. Dr. Walter Cannon found that the heart works nine hours and rests fifteen in the twenty-four. The heart works and then rests between beats. This alternation of contraction and relaxation in systole and diastole enables it to avoid fatigue and to serve us for a lifetime. In the heart are both types of muscles, but the fibers of the heart differ very remarkably from those of other striped muscles. What other set of muscles in the body serves us as well? There is no better example of complete rest alternating with forceful activity.

In the unconscious functions of bodily tissues rest is paired with work, as can also be noted in fiber-bundles within all muscles. The contracting biceps, for example, does not work as a whole, but groups of fiber-bundles keep interchanging so that one set may rest while the other works. Rest alternating with work is the secret of the balance of forces in the timing system in the human being.

CHANGING LOADS

Two of the most important and available means of relief from strains, both physiological and mechanical, are to break the focus of mental attention frequently, and to change bodily positions. If this experience is exercised in the proper spirit, habitual *fixities* in thinking may disappear; fixed muscle-patterns will be changed, and tensions thus reduced.

If one holds a fixed position too long, or performs the same act too many times, alteration in activity and rest rhythms in the muscles is lost and fatigue is present. In varying one's position at work, one may change from sitting to standing, or merely change emphasis of weight upon the chair. This will insure against habit-forming fixations of body *parts*—static contraction in the muscles; bad posture-habits. Change position of *parts* and give the reciprocal muscles a chance to shift their loads. This need applies even to the fine muscles of the eye.

Eye fatigue is frequently most devastating in such close work as reading, writing, drawing, painting. We should break the focus often, every fifteen to thirty minutes. Rest the eye muscles by becoming interested in a distant focal point. A famous eye specialist suggests that we keep our eyes on "far horizons." "Bright, piercing eyes" are always associated with seafaring folk, with mountaineers, with all out-of-door persons who are accustomed to scanning distances. When gazing at a distant object do not strain the eyes *toward it* in order to see it, but instead, *draw the object closer with your eyes.* This reduces the strain. Partially close your hand and look through it as you would a telescope, drawing the distant point *toward you* until you see it more clearly. With a little practice this will bring noticeable rest to the eyes. The pull in the eye muscles will be equalized.

FATIGUE AND DISSATISFACTIONS

Chronic fatigue may be a habit. It always contains a factor not to be found in the ordinary physical fatigue which follows healthful exercise. This hidden factor is likely to be an emotional dissatisfaction—a vague longing for something that never happens. The imagination must be cleared of such psychic habits and allowed to play upon active pictures of accomplishment. It matters not how trivial the accomplishment, as long as it engages the neuromuscular mechanism in a *positive, active manner.*

There is nothing more fatiguing for our *active behavior unit* than to be *preparing always* for something that is never consummated in *doing.* Learn to interpret sensations which come from these preparation habits, and place the causes where they belong. They lie in emotional imbalances, confusions in thinking. Change your thinking and change your physical habits. This is done through the imagination—unless you can imagine a thing taking place, it does not take place. The living organism has a great capacity for change and unity. Form the habit of frequent small, deep movements of balance-adjustments. These may be so deep-seated and so close to the joints that they are practically imperceptible. Slight shifting of weights at specific points!

PSYCHIC HABITS

There are certain fundamental responses in the body which are beyond the power of conscious effort to control. These responses are made to certain "feelings" or emotions, and we speak of such responses as psychic responses. The word "psychic" refers to feelings or emotions which influence bodily changes, both visible and invisible. Such changes in organic activity may be spoken of as psychic activity—psychic because they are ruled by feeling and not by self-determination. Dr. Walter Cannon demonstrated, for example, that gastric secretions take place in "sham feeding" in laboratory experiments in which food does not reach the stomach but the smell and sight of it give all the pleasure experienced in eating. This secretion may be spoken of as psychic secretion, taking place because of certain pleasurable sensations.

Psychic inactivity may also be produced, in which emotions or feelings, not pleasurable, inhibit the flow of gastric juices. There may also be "psychic tone" or "psychic contraction" in both surface and deep muscles. Through these psychic processes changes are made in the deep rhythms of movement and in chemical balance.

Emotions are stimulating. They produce contraction in the muscles in *preparation for movement*. Thinking is also stimulating and the muscular response is sure. The tendency to tighten or pull up the chest and neck muscles appears every day under emotional or mental strain. This may produce headaches, backaches, and other uncomfortable symptoms. These reactions come from the central reflexes and the memory patterns are a part of our inherited *preparedness for danger*. In overfatigue man holds this alerted attitude too long; he is in continuous preparation for something that never happens, is never consummated in action.

DANGER OF MUSCLE TENSIONS

Tension is a condition of the neuromuscular unit resulting from a special type of thinking and a specific type of reaction. This condition produces fatigue elements in the muscles, which persist until some change in action happens to break the specific pattern of behavior.

While in terms of mechanics tension is elongation or stretching, that which we call tension in the human body is really continuous muscular contraction due to preparations for movements which are held—inhibited, turned in.

So it comes about that fatigue lies mostly in the muscles— muscles of eyes, blood vessels, viscera, bony structure. Fatigue is due to restriction of motion, shallow breathing, inhibitory tensions. These tensions are unnecessary contractions in muscles. They serve no good purpose. The increase of poisons in the muscle fibers and in the bloodstream, and the reduction of oxygen supply to all body cells, make the fires of life an expensive process. Combustion must take place to convert the potential energy of the body into kinetic energy, its working form. Combustion produces "ash"—waste products. These must be carried off by lymph and blood, and by the breathing mechanism, and new oxygen and fuel supplied.

The parts of the body are so interrelated through the complicated nervous system that these tensions in soft tissues may cause distressing functional disturbances. Indigestion which sometimes follows persistent eyestrain is an example. More important still are the psychological reactions which hide in the unconscious to spring upon us when conditions offer an opportunity. Fatigue tensions cause vague unnamed fears.

These gripping muscles remind one of what one writer said of the "small person": "He is always hanging on to the tailboard of the wagon of progress and hollering, "Whoa!"

FATIGUE LIES IN MUSCLES

Whether the causes of fatigue are mental, emotional, or physical—and in fact these cannot be separated—tensions result. Fatigue poisons always occur first in the muscles. Before the load becomes too heavy for the blood to handle, some method of restoration should be applied. This may be done physically by changing bone balance, unlocking bones from the tense muscles gripping them; mentally, by changing thinking; emotionally, by substituting another emotional stimulus for the present one.

MOVEMENT ALTERNATION AS REST

All structures are composed of an infinite number of parts, each struggling to maintain equilibrium in a closely cooperating mechanism. The mechanical laws which control the action and reaction of the forces operating between these minute parts are accurate and definite. The manner in which these parts are maintained in relation to the whole determines the perfect or imperfect adjustment of the mechanism. Does it experience an expensive or a conservative maintenance of balance? Is it comfortable or uncomfortable?

Alternate the rest and work rhythms. The best ideas come unconsciously while the organism is at rest. Left fallow for a while, the imagination gets new creative ideas. Work rhythms then proceed unhampered.

One need not lie down to rest. Rest comes from restoring balance—mental, emotional, structural. Watch the horse in the field, detached from the plow. Meal bag suspended from neck, he sags first one hip and then the other, shaking a leg free from its fatigue tensions. He may then paw the ground gently with one forefoot after the other. Through these gentle, relaxed movements instinctively performed in an aimless kind of way, he re-establishes circulation and cell balance. By a vigorous rubdown the jockey rejuvenates his high-spirited animal after the race. The acting cells are brought back to the resting stage to regenerate.

You are immeasurably linked with the past. Nature has organized your forces into patterns of behavior for survival. Since you have survived, they too have survived.

"DRIVING" THE HUMAN MECHANISM

An intelligent automobile-driver knows that by avoiding unnecessary strains on his engine, or drains on his battery, or wear and tear on his brakes, he not only prolongs the life and efficiency of his car but makes better time on the road. There are, to be sure, many drivers who understand nothing of the machine they clumsily and wastefully handle. Some of us drive our bodies on more or less the same principle. The wise man knows that economy of operation is no more important in connection with his car, or his factory, or his office, than with his own irreplaceable body-machine.

It has been found that by applying certain familiar laws of mechanics to one's body it is possible to relieve its strains, to bring it into balance, to release its mental and physical energies into smooth, economical performance, and to maintain it in good running order, even through periods of hard usage.

To do this effectively, however, one must rest often. Rest, in the final analysis, is synonymous with equilibrium of the body parts. Learning, therefore, to restore its equilibrium after its parts have been pulled off center by the strains of the day—be these mental or physical—is essential to experience the value of *constructive rest*.

CHOICES IN PATTERNS OF REST

A most interesting question in self-analysis is whether one rests more by saving or by spending, by "stopping" or by "going." Assuming that the mechanics of life are understood and that the general aim and attitudes and their means of expression are well defined, there still remains the interesting decision regarding patterns of rest. Shall one rest by growing roses or by joining organizations, by going to sleep early or by going to meet the visiting celebrity? By resting at home reading or by going to a show? By tightening and using a little more "will," or by relaxing and having more sensory appreciation? By taking on or putting off work, by letting others open the door, or by opening the door oneself? These issues are behind the whole setup of job, avocation, and routine, and every answer comes differently. The real restorative is whatever makes one a new person, whatever restores poise to the personality.

The routine rest-fundamental of daily life is sleep. But one really rests when one *ceases to get ready to do this or that.* It is very fatiguing to remain too long in a state of preparation, for no rest comes if one fails to carry through. It has been aptly said that rest is the cessation of trying to control oneself or one's destiny.

The easier tempo of an earlier day favored *organic optimism;* life took nature's pace. Those charming fragments of the classics when the poet rests, looking over the mirror-dark sea, or sits beside the thatched cottage where bees hum, recall one of the essentials about rest. The environmental pace of nature's sight and sound flows into the organism through all its senses, almost through its pores. A restful environment makes relaxation easy, but by understanding its meaning we may attain it anywhere.

Modern man does not sit as Horace sat, looking at the landscape for renewal. The average man has no landscape; he must rest in motion. Strenuous living demands strenuous rest. While this means that rest may be intensively active—traveling, dancing, skiing—it also means that intensity may finally translate itself into the opposite, the desire for utter blankness with "inactivity of the body and emptiness of mind." In this, rest resolves ultimately into life values, inner mechanisms take over, and unity of thinking and doing is restored. The natural reaction to unstrained, pleasurable activity rehabilitates the second phase of movement, that of relaxation—the human being returned to balance, his rhythms re-established.

FACTS DEVELOP ADULTS

When we try to overcome our fatigue maladjustments, whether emotional or structural, the philosophy engendered in our deepest thinking is important. Have we learned to relate ourselves to the larger concepts of life, or are we still clinging to infantile concepts limiting both ourselves and our environments? Are we adults, or are we still infants waiting, perhaps demanding that some magic or Santa Claus arrange our lives and supply our needs? How disappointed we are doomed to be!

One need have little fear of results if one builds into the imagination facts that not only are true, but *necessary to living integrity.* Here there is no room for accusation of others, or accusation of oneself. When we learn to live in the "eternal now," we can learn to direct the sequences in our own thinking. It is astonishing how frequently and unwittingly they go awry. It requires vigilance to keep negative patterns out of the imagination. This can be accomplished only by constantly supplying new and vital images for the imagination to play upon. Focus on *positive,* factual thinking unruffled by the emotional upheavals around you and see how quickly poise and relaxation will become your habit; see how this faith in living will expand your behavior.

CHAPTER XXII

Man's Adjustment in Cosmic Order

What does it mean to grow up? It should mean that the appraising machinery of thought, reason, and judgment matures as experiences and learnings take place. Through the nerve connections between the outside and the inside, inheritance and environment meet and intertwine. Connective fibers in brain and nervous systems are the means to this end. The glands and muscles play their important parts in forming behavior patterns, organizing new ones, or strengthening those that are all ready to function at birth.

Muscles do not reason. They are parts of reflex arcs set in action by stimuli. The *cortical determinations* develop through education and through one's mental and spiritual unity in the philosophy of daily living. Self-discipline, valuable to the individual and to society, develops likewise and becomes habituated through changing the mental and emotional life by way of the imagination and movement. Change the thinking, and responses will change. The aggressive survival-patterns in the reflexes can be beneficially utilized only by intelligent action—by doing, not by thwarting or by efforts to undo.

INSTINCTS

Often instinctive reactions contradict the ideals in our thinking. The result is unhappiness and further trouble for ourselves and others. The basis of most functional nervous disturbances is retreat from difficulty, due largely to the conflict between ideals and instincts. The latter always have emotional support. When this habit of retreating from difficulty is established, one may be entirely unconscious that he is retreating from *every* difficulty. When moral pressures increase, his nervous system is caught in the vice of this habit. There is confusion in his decisions and he grows unwilling to trust them. He leans more and more heavily upon the decisions of others, and when these are lacking he is lost indeed.

Many complexities arise that confuse man's reactions as he tries to acquire the ideals of a civilized world. By inhibiting his outward expression without understanding the history of his impulses he leaves himself in an uncertain, repressed state of consciousness. Through this process of inhibition, changes are made in the deep rhythms of movement of the living body, and in the chemical substances through changes in glandular and blood supplies. The chemical changes may even extend to the very substance of the creative hormones and influence the next generation.

The psyche, or ego, of the individual is busy synthesizing all reactions registered today in relation to those registered in the past, and making ready for appropriate responses. When these are constructive, a gentle and pleasant agitation deep within gives personal assurance that whatever the responses may be they will prove adequate to the situation. One's constructive powers are built out of knowledge and faith. Find the knowledge, establish the faith, and through the imagination constructive use will be assured. A positive and poised personality results.

Conscious inhibitions are established by what man has already decided to believe. Beliefs or standards honored by time and institutions possess him. In all ages, acceptance of newly discovered facts is slow and hesitating. We need more cosmic consciousness.

COSMIC CONSCIOUSNESS

What do we mean by cosmic consciousness? It would seem to imply a *sense* of the vastness and limitlessness of time and space and the incessant struggle for balance of all forces. As we move with this thought we hold less, mentally and physically. We balance more. When imagination supported by facts and understanding takes over, we become one with the great whole. As we drop our fixities in thought and action, knowledge seems easier to attain. Facts, both spiritual and scientific, are assembled in the imagination to produce a new set of ideals, and deeper growth is possible. It is as easy to entertain facts in the imagination as fiction handed on from past generations. Seek truth and truth will operate your life. Building fiction into the imagination through wishful thinking is of no benefit to a developing personality.

Through movement the cosmos evolved. Through movement man evolved.

The cosmic order is a lawful order. Man survives through an orderly equipment. We must accept nature's laws and try to understand them. We must build mentally and spiritually upon the mechanisms given to us by the grace of God.

To contribute to better living in the world we must *accept nature;* try to appreciate what she is and what she has given to us and attend to our God-given powers for better reception, better correlation, and freer, more expansive response. We can deepen the intensity of life by enriching its reception. Thus we may learn to command and guide its responses toward less selfish ends. We can be just as spiritual when knowing the scientific facts about God's universe as when not knowing them. Science and religion have one thing at least in common—they both bring to light God's laws as they affect His universe.

As we learn more of the operation of law, we find a closer union between ourselves, nature, and God. In prayer the "I" becomes less important than formerly. We do not expect nature or God to change cosmic laws to satisfy our personal whims— our requests for more rain or more sunshine, more wealth or more comfort. These seem unimportant in relation to the whole. The answer to prayer lies in the *faith* of the individual. A great faith releases the grip of the possessive fears within. The inner-springs of wisdom come to life and become oriented with the greater purposes of life.

SPIRITUALITY

Today prayer is often conceived as an emotional experience which assists in orienting motives, purposes, and plans for better living. Acceptance enables us to get outside our little selves. To try to relate ourselves to causes and forces that are bigger than we are is a deep experience, and one of the wisest things we can do. This is the larger interpretation of prayer, and of spirituality.

The "I" seems less important today than ever before, as, in the light of new knowledge, it loses itself in the *good of the whole*. It recognizes the two great forces of the cosmos, the laws of God and the laws of nature—religion and science!

Religions, as we know them today, have all evolved from various faiths or dogmas which would seem to be the evolution of responses to "God-fearing" instincts in the breasts of man. The idea that any one particular dogma is the special guardian of spirituality seems, on the face of it, to be absurd. One of our leading scientists has said that religion is the "greatest of the conditioned reflexes." We have conditioned our own reflexes through religious education. Has spirituality kept pace with religion?

Spirituality is a universal quality. It has nothing to do with any particular faith or dogma. It may or may not appear in persons essentially religious.

An individual with a high level of cellular activity, increased sensitivity, and active responses, and with ideals to direct these responses toward unselfish ends, may be considered a spiritual person. Spiritual values lie in the high purposes of his ideals.

Such a person, acute to a high degree in his sensory reception, and purporting to direct his responding mechanisms toward social ends, would be more spiritual than one who sensed only part of his world and directed his responses to narrow or thin ends—that is, selfish ends.

One might, therefore, define spirituality as a high degree of sensitivity of the organism directed toward ends that lie outside the individual. And this irrespective of any religious order with which he might be affiliated!

Spiritual values and scientific facts may be found to work hand in hand. The facts of science act on every atom of man's substance. Spiritual awareness, with accompanying faith, acts as persistently upon his inner velocities.

We say, "God's will be done." Is not God expressing His will in the laws that He has established? Would it not be a "song of praise" to His wisdom if we acquainted ourselves with those laws and cooperated with them? There are physiological and mechanical laws, as well as psychological laws, common to all creatures. Who established these laws? How did they come about? What brought cosmic order out of chaos? We might pause to ask ourselves these questions before making final decisions about the basic qualities of either religion or spirituality.

Are all religious persons necessarily spiritual? Are all spiritual persons necessarily religious? If we honestly try to answer these two questions, we are forced to declare that these two do not necessarily coincide. Spirituality may or may not appear in persons who are secretly or openly religious. It therefore does not coincide with any particular faith or dogma.

Religion and science, the two great forces operating in life! Both carry with them obligations. Our conscience tells us that we ought to do this or that to establish "brotherly love." Our knowledge of natural law tells us that we ought to do this or that to establish a keener consciousness of law and order. The more truth we have discovered in both religion and science, the greater is our own responsibility.

Before we have learned that "telling lies" may do harm to others and that taking something that does not belong to us certainly does harm to others, we have not developed a conscience. After we know the truth about these two social offenses and still have not developed a conscience but continue in our former behavior, the law may take us over. After we learn that fire burns and bones break, if we continue to play carelessly with fire and jump from high places to land on hard surfaces, the hospital may take us over. Both conscience and physical well-being strengthen with the development of constructive habits.

Harry Nelson Wieman, in *The Wrestle of Religion with Truth,* says, "One of the best habits to form is the habit of forming habits in ever greater number. This is growth; this is progress. Growth depends upon forming this supremely generative, regulative habit. By forming new habits all the time and adding them to the old, the individual progressively increases the range and fullness of his interaction with the total environment. Thus he increases the abundance of his life."

The art of living is expressed in finding unity and meaning in the great variety of our expanded sensory field, the intricate correlations and the appropriate responses.

We might speculate on the words of Henry Drummond on the possibilities of man's future evolution having a "future as great as its past. . . . So stupendous is the development from the atom to the man that no point can be fixed in the future so distant from what man is now as he is from the atom. . . . Evolution being found in so many different sciences, the likelihood is that it is a universal principle."

We are viewing life as an expression of the directions and velocities of cellular protoplasm in the responses of man's organism as a whole. One who can interpret what the world says to him, and can respond with increased satisfaction as his experiences enlarge, has found unity in life.

CPSIA information can be obtained
at www.ICGtesting.com
Printed in the USA
BVHW031044171221
624277BV00003B/198